Communications
in Computer and Information Science

1594

More information about this series at https://link.springer.com/bookseries/7899

Enrique Gonzalez · Mariela Curiel ·
Andrés Moreno · Angela Carrillo-Ramos ·
Rafael Páez · Leonardo Flórez-Valencia (Eds.)

Advances in Computing

15th Colombian Congress, CCC 2021
Bogotá, Colombia, November 22–26, 2021
Revised Selected Papers

 Springer

Editors
Enrique Gonzalez ⓘ
Pontificia Universidad Javeriana
Bogotá, Colombia

Andrés Moreno ⓘ
Pontificia Universidad Javeriana
Bogotá, Colombia

Rafael Páez ⓘ
Pontificia Universidad Javeriana
Bogotá, Colombia

Mariela Curiel ⓘ
Pontificia Universidad Javeriana
Bogotá, Colombia

Angela Carrillo-Ramos ⓘ
Pontificia Universidad Javeriana
Bogotá, Colombia

Leonardo Flórez-Valencia ⓘ
Pontificia Universidad Javeriana
Bogotá, Colombia

ISSN 1865-0929   ISSN 1865-0937 (electronic)
Communications in Computer and Information Science
ISBN 978-3-031-19950-9   ISBN 978-3-031-19951-6 (eBook)
https://doi.org/10.1007/978-3-031-19951-6

This Springer imprint is published by the registered company Springer Nature Switzerland AG
The registered company address is: Gewerbestrasse 11, 6330 Cham, Switzerland

Preface

The Colombian Computing Society (SCo2 for its acronym in Spanish) was founded in 2005 in order to contribute to the development of research in Colombia and to facilitate the relationship between researchers related to computer science, not only within the country but also worldwide. The most important event of the SCo2 is the Colombian Congress of Computing (CCC). This volume presents the papers of the 15th CCC event held in 2021. This congress was organized by the Pontificia Universidad Javeriana, with the support of RENATA, the National Academic Network of Advanced Technology.

CCC 2021 marked the return of the series, after its interruption in 2020 due to the COVID-19 pandemic situation. Indeed, it was not easy to resume organizing the congress when the health conditions had not yet returned to normal. Due to this atypical situation, the size of the event was moderate and it was held completely remotely, for the first time. Despite the limitations, we managed to move the CCC series forward and revived this meeting place for computer researchers, not only from Colombia but also from other countries.

CCC 2021 received 47 submissions which were sent for peer review. Only eight full papers and two short papers were accepted; thus, the acceptation rate was 17%. For the paper evaluation, a double-blind system was used. The average number of reviews per paper was 3.1 and the average number of papers assigned to a reviewer was 1.39. All the accepted papers were revised after the event. The 10 accepted articles were organized into three main themes: Artificial intelligence, Educational Informatics, and Information Systems.

Although CCC 2021 was small in size, the papers presented were of high quality, once again demonstrating the contribution that computer science can make to solve high-impact problems. We thank all the people and institutions that supported the development of the event, especially the peer reviewers for their invaluable work. We hope that with this event, there will be a rebirth of the cooperation and participation of researchers and partner institutions in SCo2.

November 2022

Enrique González
Mariela Curiel
Andrés Moreno
Angela Carrillo-Ramos
Rafael Páez
Leonardo Flórez

Organization

General Chair

Enrique Gonzalez   Pontificia Universidad Javeriana, Colombia

Program Committee Chairs

Cardozo Nicolás	Universidad de los Andes, Colombia
Duque Néstor	Universidad Nacional de Colombia, Colombia
Flórez-Valencia Leonardo	Pontificia Universidad Javeriana, Colombia
Gómez María Clara	Universidad de Medellín, Colombia
Ruiz Pablo	Corporación Universitaria Comfacauca, Colombia
Sanabria Ordoñez John Alexander	Universidad del Valle, Colombia
Solano Andrés	Universidad Autónoma de Occidente, Colombia
Tabares Betancur Marta Silvia	Universidad EAFIT, Colombia
Vargas Montoya Héctor Fernando	ITM, Colombia

Steering Committee

Mariela Curiel	Pontificia Universidad Javeriana, Colombia
Andrés Moreno	Pontificia Universidad Javeriana, Colombia
Angela Carrillo-Ramos	Pontificia Universidad Javeriana, Colombia
Rafael Páez	Pontificia Universidad Javeriana, Colombia
Leonardo Flórez	Pontificia Universidad Javeriana, Colombia

Program Committee

Aballay Laura	Universidad Nacional de San Juan, Argentina
Agredo Delgado Vanessa	Universidad del Cauca, Colombia
Álvarez Jiménez Charlems	Universidad Nacional de Colombia, Colombia
Arango Lopez Jeferson	Universidad de Caldas, Colombia
Avila Gabriel	Institución Universitaria Politécnico Grancolombiano, Colombia
Bacca Acosta Jorge Luis	University of Girona, Spain
Balocco Simone	Universitat de Barcelona, Spain
Barber Federico	Universitat Politècnica de València, Spain
Bucheli Víctor	Universidad del Valle, Colombia
Calderón Bocanegra Francisco Carlos	Pontificia Universidad Javeriana, Colombia

Camacho Marta	Institución Universitaria Colegio Mayor del Cauca, Colombia
Cano Sandra	Pontificia Universidad Católica de Valparaíso, Chile
Cardona Sergio	Universidad del Quindio, Colombia
Carrillo-Ramos Angela	Pontificia Universidad Javeriana, Colombia
Castellanos Eduardo	Pontificia Universidad Javeriana, Colombia
Castillo Luis Fernando	Universidad de Caldas, Colombia
Castrillon Helder	Corporación Universitaria Comfacauca, Colombia
Castro Rojas Luis Fernando	Universidad del Quindío, Colombia
Cerón Magaly	Corporación Universitaria de Comfacauca, Colombia
Challiol Cecilia	Universidad Nacional de La Plata, Argentina
Chavarriaga Jaime	Universidad de Los Andes, Colombia
Chavarro Porras Julio César	Universidad Tecnológica de Pereira, Colombia
Collazos César	Universidad del Cauca, Colombia
Cortés-Rico Laura	Universidad Militar Nueva Granada, Colombia
Cruz Angel Alfonso	Universidad de los Llanos, Colombia
Curiel Mariela	Pontificia Universidad Javeriana, Colombia
Del Giorgio Horacio	Universidad Nacional de La Matanza, Argentina
Díaz Jaime	Universidad de La Frontera, Chile
Esparza Maldonado Alma Laura	Instituto de Investigación, Desarrollo e Innovación en Tecnologías Interactivas, Mexico
Fernández Alejandro	Universidad Nacional de La Plata, Argentina
Flores-Rios Brenda L.	Universidad Autónoma de Baja California, Mexico
Franco Triana Hugo	Universidad Central, Colombia
Gamess Eric	Jacksonville State University, USA
García-Alonso Jose	University of Extremadura, Spain
Gil-Herrera Juliver	ITM, Colombia
Gonzalez Enrique	Pontificia Universidad Javeriana, Colombia
Grigera Julián	Universidad Nacional de La Plata, Argentina
Guerrero Garcia Josefina	Benemérita Universidad Autónoma de Puebla, Mexico
Gutiérrez Ricardo	Universidad Militar Nueva Granada, Colombia
Gómez Sebastián	Tecnológico de Antioquia, Colombia
Gómez Mora Miller	Universidad Distrital Francisco José de Caldas, Colombia
Gómez-Morantes Juan E.	Pontificia Universidad Javeriana, Colombia
Hernandez Juliana	Universidad de Medellín, Colombia
Hurtado Julio	Universidad del Cauca, Colombia
Isaza Gustavo	Universidad de Caldas, Colombia
Julian Vicente	Universitat Politècnica de València, Spain

Lago Paula	Universidad Nacional Abierta y a Distancia, Colombia
Leal Emilcy	Universidad de Medellín, Colombia
Lliteras Alejandra Beatriz	Universidad Nacional de La Plata, Argentina
Luna-García Huizilopoztli	Universidad Autónoma de Zacatecas, Mexico
Marino Olga	Universidad de los Andes, Colombia
Molina Díaz Ana Isabel	University of Castilla-La Mancha, Spain
Mon Alicia	Universidad Nacional de La Matanza, Argentina
Montero Anabel	Pontificia Universidad Javeriana, Colombia
Montoya Maria	Universidad Tecnológica de Pereira, Colombia
Montoya Múnera Edwin	Universidad EAFIT, Colombia
Moreno Andrés	Pontificia Universidad Javeriana, Colombia
Moreno Julian	Universidad Nacional de Colombia, Colombia
Muñoz Sanabria Luis Freddy	Fundación Unversitaria de Popayan, Colombia
Méndez Yenny	Universidad Mayor de Chile, Chile
Ortega Cantero Manuel	University of Castilla-La Mancha, Spain
Osorio Germán	Universidad Nacional de Colombia, Colombia
Paderewski Patricia	University of Granada, Spain
Pomares Quimbaya Alexandra	Pontificia Universidad Javeriana, Colombia
Pastrana Manuel	Universidad San Buenaventura, Colombia
Pavón Juan	Universidad Complutense de Madrid, Spain
Paz Freddy	Pontificia Universidad Católica del Perú, Perú
Peláez Valencia Luis Eduardo	EDU-SQA S.A.S., Colombia
Puertas Edwin	Universidad Tecnológica de Bolívar, Colombia
Páez Rafael	Pontificia Universidad Javeriana, Colombia
Quiza-Montealegre Jhon Jair	Universidad de Medellín, Colombia
Quiñones Otey Daniela	Pontificia Universidad Católica de Valparaíso, Chile
Ramírez Mauricio	Universidad de Medellín, Colombia
Rodríguez Marín Paula Andrea	Universidad Nacional de Colombia, Colombia
Rueda Olarte Andrea del Pilar	Pontificia Universidad Javeriana, Colombia
Sarmiento Wilson J.	Universidad Militar Nueva Granada, Colombia
Sarria M. Gerardo M.	Pontificia Universidad Javeriana, Cali, Colombia
Sepúlveda Lina	Universidad de Medellín, Colombia
Sepúlveda Rodríguez Luis Eduardo	Universidad del Quindío, Colombia
Serra-Ruiz Jordi	Universitat Oberta de Catalunya, Spain
Silveira Ricadro	Universidade Federal de Santa Catarina, Brazil
Silvestre Luis	Universidad de Talca, Chile
Solórzano Giovanny Piedrahita	Institución Universitaria Politécnico Grancolombiano, Colombia
Torres Diego	Universidad Nacional de La Plata, Argentina

Vicari Rosa	Universidade Federal do Rio Grande do Sul, Brazil
Villegas Maria	Universidad del Quindío, Colombia
Vivas Aurelio	Universidad de los Andes, Colombia
Vélez Gloria	Universidad Pontificia Bolivariana, Colombia
Zapata Jaramillo Carlos Mario	Universidad Nacional de Colombia, Colombia

Organizing Institutions

Contents

Artificial Intelligence

SIMALL: Emotional BDI Model for Customer Simulation in a Mall

Daniel S. Valencia[1], Jairo E. Serrano[2]([⊠]) [iD], and Enrique Gonzalez[1] [iD]

[1] Pontificia Universidad Javeriana, Bogotá, Colombia
{daniel.valencia,egonzal}@javeriana.edu.co
[2] Universidad Tecnológica de Bolívar, Cartagena, Colombia
jserrano@utb.edu.co

Abstract. Modeling customer behavior and exploring the motivations that drive their actions within a shopping mall is the subject of study in multiple works, which has generated new theories in marketing and related areas. However, seen from a computational perspective, the modeling of this system is complex given its emergent behavioral nature. In this paper, we propose a decision support model through a simulation implemented with multi-agent systems emphasizing the emotional BDI model and fuzzy logic decision making. This simulator is used to recognize improvement opportunities for businesses operation within a shopping mall.

Keywords: Shopping centers · Agent-based simulator · Emotional BDI · Customer simulation · Mall simulation · Purchasing intention

1 Introduction

The constant search for and retention of satisfied and profitable customers is a condition of success for most businesses. Although an individual's financial spending behavior is commonly labeled as irrational; thus, understanding and modeling customer behavior can provide strategic business analysts with a better understanding of how customers make purchasing decisions and, more importantly, also realize and assess how these decisions can be influenced. The customer's decision-making mechanism is complex and non-deterministic. In addition, it must include the resolution of conflicts between emotional and experiential impulses. In this work, a rational agent that incorporates emotional human like decision mechanisms, based on fuzzy logic, in order to simulate customers in a mall simulator is introduced.

In this context, for the design and development of the shopping center simulator, a decision making model inspired by the practical reasoning of humans, proposed by Michael Bratman [6], was implemented. In this model, customers are represented as BDI (Belief, Desire, and Intention) agents, with the particularity that their beliefs represent the knowledge of the world with which they interact and they achieve their goals through the execution of actions related to

© Springer Nature Switzerland AG 2022
E. Gonzalez et al. (Eds.): CCC 2021, CCIS 1594, pp. 3–18, 2022.
https://doi.org/10.1007/978-3-031-19951-6_1

their intentions. Since the emotional factor is one of the most influential aspects in the customers' purchase decision-making process, an emotional model was implemented to represent multiple conditions or situations that generate emotional stimuli. Then, according to the resulting level of intensity in the agent's emotional state, a positive or negative, intense or subtle influence is generated, which directly influences the decision making processes.

This paper delves into the BDI model of the customer agent in the SIMALL simulator. The first section presents in the state of art, a review of the buyer influence model, the BDI models, and some emotional models. Section two presents the proposed BDI model for the customer agent and explains in detail the beliefs, desires, and intentions of the this agent, the main one of multi-agent system (MAS) based simulator. In section three, the decision-making mechanism based on fuzzy logic and the buyer's emotional model are presented. The last two sections are include the results and conclusions.

2   State of Art

This section provides a summary of the concepts and models that support the conceptual framework underpinning the model proposed in this article. First, the selected buying influence model is presented; then, the bases of the agent architecture for simulation and the BDI agents that inspire this work are established. Finally, the emotional models and the cognitive process bases for the calculation of the agent's emotional state are described.

2.1   Purchasing Influence Model

Several models allow representing the factors that influence purchase intention. Ali and Moulin built a virtual mall to test the behavior of potential customers concerning products, comparing the behavior with real data collected in several shopping malls [2]. On the other hand, Burke explored how customers allocate their attention in a complex and competitive environment and assess the impact of store factors on shopper behavior [8]. These experiences do not make use of agents or emotions. However, they served as the basis for the realization of the agent-based simulation described below.

In this work, the AIDA model [9] was implemented. It presents a modern marketing and advertising theory based on consumer perception. AIDA (Attention, Interest, Desire, and Action) describes a standard list of stages (see Fig. 1) that can occur when a consumer engages with an advertisement. The Attention stage intents to increment awareness by attracting the customer's attention to the products; then, the Interest stage seeks to increase the customer's interest by focusing on and demonstrating the advantages and benefits (rather than focusing on the features of the product or service, as in traditional marketing); the Desire stage convinces customers that they want and desire the product or service and that it will satisfy their needs. Finally, the Action stage directs customers to take the purchase of the product.

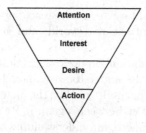

Fig. 1. AIDA model decision pyramid

Based on the AIDA model, the objective of marketing is to attract the attention of potential customers and arouse their interest and desire for the final purchase action. By executing this process step by step, the total number of potential customers decreases, and seen from the perspective of convincing power, the base number of customers becomes an inverted pyramid. The marketing strategy of this model generally seeks to enlarge the bottom of the triangle or increase the conversion rate to obtain real customers. The most important constraint of this model suggests that enlarging the bottom of the triangle will increase the cost of marketing. Inconsistency between marketing and customer needs will reduce the conversion rate to gain entry into the next layer of the AIDA model.

The generic model for purchase decision-making, summarized by Bray [7] based on Engel-Blackwell-Miniard Model, consists of five major phases, each composed of different activities and actions. The first phase is identifying the need, in which the consumer identifies an imbalance between his current state and the desired state. The second phase is searching for information, in which an exploration of alternatives to satisfy the need is carried out. The third phase is the evaluation of alternatives, in which the information collected is used to establish selection criteria. The fourth phase is the purchase and delivery, which consists of executing the purchase process through the exchange of payment with the delivery of the product or service. Finally, the fifth phase is the post-purchase evaluation, which consists of making general use of the product or service and an evaluation of the functionality. This process relates to the following customer states in the decision-making process: initiator, influencer, decision-maker, buyer, and user. This general purchase process allows the definition of the underlying sub-processes and the identification of the elements of the purchase simulation model for customers in a shopping mall.

2.2 BDI Agent-Based Simulation

"Simulation, in general, is one of the most powerful analytical tools available", posited a 1975 compilation study of the state of the art by Shannon [20] highlighting its applicability in a wide range of application areas. Simulation research and its applicability are still ongoing, being supported by computational sciences [21]. The possibilities provided have been strengthened with powerful working tools and theories that facilitate research, reaching higher levels of accuracy, achieving better modeling of the real world, and generating simulations that help in decision making.

In the field of Social Simulation, Squazzoni [22] describes how social dynamics and behavioral patterns can be understood by modeling at the micro-scale (the individuals represented by agents), and at the macro-scale (the social fabric represented in the interaction between agents). By studying the relationship between the micro and the macro, an understanding of social phenomena can be achieved, giving way to various types of applications, for instance: how to make investments [5], analysis of the movement of people in open or closed spaces [13] or understanding the behavior and decisions of people inside a shopping mall [11].

A widely used methodology in social simulation is the use of agents, defining an agent as an entity that perceives its environment, being able to react to it, that can communicate or cooperate with peers, and that by working in a coordinated manner can solve various types of problems [4]. To make decisions autonomously and rationally, prioritizing objectives, the proposed model is based on a BDI architecture. This architecture is implemented and complemented with an emotional model for decision making. This integration, between the BDI and the emotional models, allows to deal with a wide range of applications [1]. These features facilitate the implementation of the AIDA model, presented earlier. In fact, the AIDA model and the BDI architecture are inspired by human reasoning processes; therefore, its implementation and integration is highly cohesive during the simulator development process.

2.3   Emotional Models

There are multiple implementations of agent-based emotional models, one of these is Affective computing [14]; it seeks to develop systems that can recognize, interpret, process, and simulate human affect. In this sense, there have been several implementations of emotional models based on multi-agent systems that use the BDI architecture inspired by the way of thinking of human beings.

Hu [12] proposes a BDI agent model with an emotional agent structure. First, it establishes a new knowledge base by applying granular computation to represent emotional expressions; then, it proposes a method to achieve emotional goals by applying rules from the knowledge base; finally, it implements emotional processing. It should be noted that the implementation was performed as an extension to the BDI model that incorporates an emotional knowledge base taken into account for the decision-making process. Moga [16] proposes an emotional model based on agents and the Control-Value theory focused on psycho-pedagogy as part of the design of an Affective Tutoring System (ATS). This proposal seeks to provide a platform for the adaptation of an individualized teaching strategy considering the emotional state of students, where its intention is focused on identifying negative inactive emotions (boredom, frustration, and hopelessness).

The previous work is based on the OCC emotional model proposed by Ortony [17]. In this model, the authors focus on the analysis of the emotional influence of agents, objects, and events. The conception of events is very simple, they are simply perceptions that individuals have about things that happen, regardless of the beliefs they may have about possible causes. Objects are elements of the world and agents are entities that, considered from the perspective of their current instruments, focus on the causes and context associated with emotional events. The influence of events on agents is not limited to persons. Agents can be influenced by animate beings, inanimate beings, or abstractions, such as institutions, and even situations perceived in a particular context. In the following section, a brief description of the OCCr [19] model that facilitates the computational implementation of the proposed emotional conceptual model is given.

2.4 Cognitive Process of Emotions

One of the most representative authors of the emotional models is Mandler [15], who suggests that what is known as "cognitive interpretation" or "meaning analysis", for example, appraisal, is the "cold" part of emotion. The "hot" part is provided by arousal, which is usually caused by the interruption of plans or sequences of actions. Mandler's theory is more attractive for this research than other arousal theories because it mainly concerns the valuational aspect of emotions and its explicit recognition of the importance of plans, goals, and knowledge representations. According to OCC, the modeling of emotion change is implemented by an arousal-based mechanism that simultaneously registers valence. This obviates the need to postulate distinct mechanisms corresponding to arousal and valence, eliminating the need to explain how these mechanisms interact with the ordinary experience of emotion.

The OCCr model inspired the emotional model adopted in this work. In our OCC approach, we propose to establish a new hierarchy, more intuitive than the one proposed in the original OCCr, where the concept of inheritance is applied, being easier to implement it in a computational model, solving the possible ambiguities and shortcomings of OCC. Emotions are implemented as events constructed from the representation of tuples of three elements: types of the occurred event, involved agents in the situation, and objects or context. The agent's emotion level will be modified depending on each one of these elements. For instance, the event "my mother wins the lotter" is represented as [win, my mother, lottery], as all three elements are positive, the happiness of the agent will increase; moreover, as the importance of these elements is high, the happiness increment will be also high.This representation allows modeling different events that resemble those experienced by customers in a shopping mall and will constitute the most critical emerging factor in the simulator.

3 SIMALL: BDI Model for Customer Simulation in a Mall

For the analysis and design of the multi-agent model proposed for the simulation, the AOPOA [18] agent-oriented programming methodology based on an organizational approach was used. The systematic AOPOA's goals decomposition process simplifies the design of complex systems. This iterative and recursive decomposition process, at the same time, identifies the interactions between the entities that compose the system.

3.1   MAS Model

The application of AOPOA decomposition of the problem, based on the objectives, assures the achievement of the overall system goals. In the context of this work, the main objective of this methodology is to identify the main agents, representing actors and entities in the simulated system, their competencies and the resources needed to achieve their objectives. The obtained MAS model also includes the formal specification of the interactions between the agents. The implementation of the model was carried out using the BESA agent platform [10]; BESA is a Java library used to easily build event driven multi-agent systems; it also includes an extension for BDI rational agents.

The multi-agent system represented in Fig. 2 is composed of five social entities: Customer, Seller, Commerce, Provider and a complimentary Manager (see Table 1). The system has other attached entities that allow greater precision in the simulation listed in the Table 2.

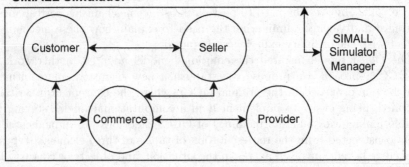

Fig. 2. SIMALL - MAS agents and interactions

The proposed MAS is defined by different entities. Customers are represented by BDI agents who are aware of their environment and interact with the entities to affect their state and carry out decision-making processes. The mall represents the world of the MAS and constitutes the environment where customers interact with the other entities: Mall, Places, Corridors, and Walls (Table 2). In the next section, the description of the Customer is made; since it must make decisions imitating the human reasoning process, this agent was designed with the BDI architecture, to achieve greater fidelity to human behavior in the real world.

Table 1. Agents of SIMALL MAS

Agent	Description
Customer	Satisfy your needs
Seller	Persuade customers to execute commercial transactions within the business they represent
Provider	Provisioning of commercial premises
Commerce	Hosting customers to make sales
Simulation Manager	Control simulation life cycle

Table 2. Complementary Entities of the SIMALL MAS

Entity	Description
Simulation Manager	Control simulation lifecycle, generates simulation reports
Shopping Center	It is the world of simulation, where interactions take place
Places	Abstract representation of the internal spaces of the shopping center
Corridors	Abstract representation of the mall's internal communication channels
Walls	They represent dividing lines between stores, corridors and restrooms
Products and services	Merchandise that is sold to customers
Quotation	Offer to customers of products or services
Categories	Classification of products in the market
Demographic context	Customer segmentation system according to demographics
Economic Context	Segmentation of customers according to their economic status
Buyer's context	Define criteria for quotation selection
Needs	Products or services required by customers
Interests	Emphasis of customers towards a certain product or service
Emotional Component	Establishes levels of intensity of emotions experienced by the customer at the time of purchase

3.2 Customer Agent BDI Model

The most important agent in the simulator is the Customer, which was designed based on a BDI architecture. The proposed is supported on a priority pyramidal goal structure. According to the analysis of performance, adaptability, and interoperability requirements, the BDI-CHA architecture organizes and orchestrates the evaluation and achievement of the agent's goals. BDI-CHA, like its predecessors, is based on the three key concepts: Beliefs, Desires, and Intentions. The difference is that these three concepts are implemented as a set of internal cooperative autonomous proactive agents. In fact, a BDI-CHA agent is a small multi-agent system; thus, the tasks related to believes updating, goals evaluation, and plans execution are performed using multiple threads running concurrently. Internal events are used to coordinate the parallel update of beliefs, the evaluation of multiple goals at the same time, and the control of the actions of plans associated to concurrent intentions.

In conclusion, the BDI-CHA architecture proposes a parallel implementation of the BDI abstract model that can improve the response time and allows implementing more complex agents. Considering the BDI-CHA model, the goals associated to the beliefs, desires, and intentions of the Customer agent were defined as summarized in Table 3.

Table 3. Goals classification

Priority	Name	Description
Survival	Feeding	Related to the level of hunger that customers may experience during their visit to the mall
Survival	Going To The Restroom	Just like eating, the physiological need to use restrooms is a physiological need
Obligation	Satisfying Needs	Encompasses the agents main goal
Opportunity	Buy	This goal seeks to identify the ideal conditions to make a purchase
Opportunity	Exit	This goal is triggered when the customer has failed to satisfy a survival need, or ended up
Opportunity	Using Banking Services	There is a type of need related to using banking services within the mall
Requirement	Quote Need	Identify stores that can meet the need and request quotes from them
Requirement	Move to Location	Transfers the customer between different locations in the mall
Requirement	Request Information	Provide the customer with the required route for travel
Requirement	Withdraw Cash	Locate the bank of your convenience and perform the cash withdrawal procedure
Need	Wander	Allows the customer to explore the mall and visit stores that match their interests

3.3 Beliefs and Desires

Beliefs are defined based on the perception of the shopping center environment in which the agent is immersed. In the case of the customer beliefs, they are further characterized by making use of the following entities: demographic, economic, and shopper data (see Table 2). Beliefs, in addition to the agent location within the mall and the routes necessary for its movement, also incorporate the emotional state and information used by the decision-making mechanisms. Moreover, the BDI-CHA's beliefs mechanism makes each goal to calculate its activation level and its contribution to the agent's global goal.

Desires represent the agent's motivational state. They model the goals or situations that an agent "would like" to achieve. A goal is a desire that the agent is interested in actively achieving. The use of the term goal consequently adds new restrictions, the set of active desires must be consistent. For example, the goals "go home" and "stay at the mall" cannot be active concurrently, even if both may be desirable. The Customer's possible desires are the result of applying the goal decomposition of the AOPOA methodology. These goals, together with the definitions obtained from the AIDA model, allowed defining the pyramidal structure of goals (see Fig. 3), which are described in the Table 3. The evaluation of all the goals is carried out proactively and in parallel. This evaluation makes it possible to determine which goals are activated and become desires. In BDI-CHA, only active goals have their contribution calculated in order to evaluate, taking into account the current state of the agent, which goals can generate the greatest benefit for the agent.

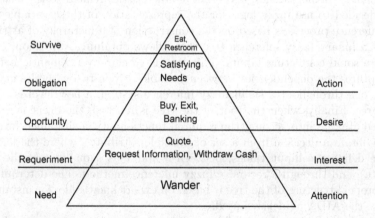

Fig. 3. Pyramidal Goals based on BDI (*left*) and AIDA model (*right*).

3.4 Intentions

Intentions represent the agent's deliberative state and correspond to active goals that are located higher in the pyramid hierarchy and also have a higher level of contribution. Intentions are desires about which the agent commits to achieve.

This means that the agent must initiate the execution of a plan. Plans are sequences of actions that an agent can perform to achieve an intention. Plans are initially conceived in partial form and progressively completed in detail, based on the believes, during their execution. The Intention is distinguished as an attitude of behavioral control. It defines commitment as the distinguishing factor between desire and intention. This leads to temporary persistence in initial plans and in other plans that are built based on those to which commitment has already been established.

An important feature of BDI-CHA model is that during the execution of a goal, other goals can be evaluated and activated simultaneously, which, through a controlled process of expropriation, takes control of the agent's behavior. In the context of SIMALL, it is the case in which during the execution of the purchase process, a new need is generated that overlaps the current need. In this case, when the persistence level of the goal exceeds the acceptance threshold, it will take control of the execution thread and impose itself on the other goals through an expropriation process.

4   Customer Fuzzy Decision and Emotional Model

The main decision-making process of the system is related to the evaluation of the variables concerned to a purchase process. This process involves multiple variables such as product cost/benefit, product quality, customer service level, brand representation in the market, customer's emotional state, among others.

Taking into account that the combination of variables can change according to personality, demographics, and other characteristics related to the customer, it was decided to use fuzzy logic for the representation of these variables. The fuzzy inference process is based on the construction of a hierarchy of attributes forming a binary fuzzy inference tree that allows obtaining a decision, even if there are some conflicting inputs. This tree is similar to a semantic network, that captures the dependencies between variables, when two variables generate another one throughout a small fuzzy inference system, a new level is created in the tree. Finally, when the root of the tree is reached, the decision value is produced. Taking into account the required functionality, a simplified form was used to obtain a decision from a set of multiple attributes, where the leaves of the tree define the input values, between 0 and 1 as a qualifier of the input attributes, and through a recursive fuzzy inference method. The determination of the proper structure of the tree is based on expert knowledge; for instance, in this case the AIDA model was used.

This fuzzy solution allows the dynamic assessment of multiple variables easily interchangeable in configuration time through a descriptor file. On the other hand, one of the attributes to be taken into account in the decision-making process is the emotional component. In order to model customer emotions, an adaptation of the emotional model proposed in the work RoboAct [3] was performed. This model allows to define a discrete set of emotional axes, each representing the polarity of opposite emotions. Each emotional axis represents the positive or negative valence of the emotion; therefore, each emotional axis has opposite poles (e.g.

Happiness/Sadness, Love/Hate, etc.). For each one of the axes, the valuation of the emotions is presented under a continuous range of values from −1 to 1; for instance, 1 can represent total happiness and −1 total sadness, all the positive values are associated with some level of happiness and the negative values represent some level of sadness. Additionally, each axis has a baseline value that can be configured for each agent in order to represent the default emotional value defined by the particular character or personality. That is, a happy person might have a baseline of 0.7 on an emotional axis where the positive pole represents happiness. Emotional levels are affected by emotional events that the agent receives when it interacts with other agents and evolves in the environment. An emotional event, as proposed by our OCC model is defined by three values: events, people, and objects. Each event is valued according to pre-established semantics for each element of the tuple. That is to say, affinity relationships between people can cause that the same event coming from different people or objects can generate different valuations. To illustrate this with an example, we have the event in which a father makes a joke to her son. In this case, given the semantics of the relationship between father and son that could be valued as Familiar or Close, it causes the event to be desirable. While the same event between teacher and student, where the semantics of the relationship is valued as Formal, causes the event to be undesirable in order to maintain that formality. Thus, for the case of the shopping mall, this emotional model generates information included among the beliefs of the agents and in this way the emotional state can be used in the decision-making process. The emotional events implemented in the mall simulator are related to the exchange of advertising messages between the stores, their showcases, sales drivers, and the customers.

5   Results

This section will describe how the experiment was conducted to test and validate the proper functioning of the shopping mall simulator. First, it will explain how the experiment was set up and then the results will be analyzed and discussed.

5.1   Design of the Experiment

Taking into account the definition of the problem, the customer behavior was modeled by taking real data from the businesses operating within an existing shopping center. For this purpose, a series of visits were made to the Calima Shopping Center in the city of Bogota to take a statistical sample of some performance variables of the commercial premises. The obtained result is a triangular distribution of the relevant performance variables (minimum, aver- age and maximum value) for the behavior of customers, such as:

- Time of permanence inside the stores
- Number of sales made in a day
- Amount of sales made per day

– Diversity in the supply of products and/or services.

Using these collected information, the simulator was calibrated and the consumption behavior of customers was configured concerning these supply and demand variables. The validation was performed by comparing the results of the simulation with the events of the real shopping mall. The proposed approach expresses the three phenomena that are known to common to shopping malls, the first one: the level of sales of the stores in the shopping center is directly proportional to the purchasing power of the customers who visit it; second one: the level of sales of the stores within the mall is directly related to the number of needs of the customers who visit the mall. And, the third one: the clustered distribution of stores speeds up the purchasing process and increases the number of sales over time vs. random distribution because the customers' travel time to make quotations is shorter.

To design the simulation experiment, performance variables were taken into account to verify that the construction of the simulation model adjusts to basic behavioral conditions in two specific scenarios, clustered or randomly located stores, as seen in Table 4. To carry out these scenarios, the experimental dependent variables were defined, which correspond to the resulting variables that will allow evaluating the performance of the test. Also, the independent variables were defined, which correspond to those that, according to their variations, allow configuring different test scenarios. Finally, the intervening variables correspond to those that directly or indirectly affect the scenario but whose configuration will not change in any of the scenarios to be tested during the experiments that were carried out and therefore have a constant value.

5.2   Results Analysis

Each experiment runs 10 times the simulation, with 8 hours of real-time time for each tested scenario. The obtained results are summarized in Table 5. It was possible to demonstrate a good performance of the model, which implies that the simulator does represent the most representative phenomena in shopping malls and the statistical tests show that they comply with this behavior.

The two scenarios were configured with the same amount of money and needs by changing the distribution of commercial stores in a clustered or random way. Figures 4 and 5 show the aisles in blue and the stores that received the most purchases in dark red circles. When there is a higher number of visits and turnover of people, it is visualized with a light red and green background.

As a result, in Fig. 4 we can observe the behavior when the physical distribution of the stores was clustered, this means that there are stores of the same type consecutively. It was found that if the stores are arranged in a condensed or clustered mode, customers move less and there is a higher volume of sales. In Table 5 we can observe a higher amount of sales whenever the stores are in clustered mode. Regardless of the needs are high or low or even if the money is low.

Table 4. Design of the experiment inside the shopping center.

Kind	Description	Values
Dependent Variables		
Quantity	Sales successfully completed	?
Independent Variables		
Purchasing Capacity	Amount of Customer's money	[Low] - Capacity below 100.000, [High] - Above 2'000.000 COP
Needs	Number of needs a customer comes to the mall with	[Low] - less than 3, [High] - more than 20
Distribution of Premises	Organization and physical distribution of stores	[Clustered] - Niche are grouped in the same location, [Randomized] - Niche are randomly dispersed
Intervening Variables		
Demographics	Variables that define the customer profile associated with the product categories offered	Age Ranges, Genders, Socio-economic Levels, Occupations and Schooling
Corridors	Corresponds to the number of vertices over which the commercial center is distributed	5
Aisles per corridor	The number of aisles separating the corridors	4
Total simulation time	Time equivalent to the actual time simulated in each run	8
Categories	Allow to classify the products offered by the stores, in this case a constant number of categories will be used	237
Stores	They offer products of one or several categories, for this case a constant amount of stores will be handled	13
Products	Products are associated to the categories and are offered by the stores. In this case, a constant number of products to be offered will be managed	103
Entrances	The mall entrances are the places where customers enter and exit the mall	1
Restrooms	Places where customers go to satisfy their need to use the restroom	2
Information Points	Information points are consulted by some customers when they do not know the location of certain stores. In this case, a constant number of information points will be managed	2

Table 5. Results

Money	Needs	Distribution	Average sales
High	High	Clustered	957
High	High	Random	882
High	Low	Clustered	584
High	Low	Random	443
Low	High	Clustered	74
Low	High	Random	65
Low	Low	Clustered	37
Low	Low	Random	32

Fig. 4. SIMALL scenario results: clustered assign commerce's.

Fig. 5. SIMALL scenario results: random assign commerce's.

On the other hand, when the distribution is random, as shown in Fig. 5, travel times increase, inter-appointment times go up and sales decrease directly. Confirming that it is better to arrange the stores in a clustered way.

6   Conclusions

The developed SIMALL simulator significantly reproduces the behavior of a shopping mall. Therefore, it was possible to confirm the hypotheses and validate the behavioral model designed. The simulator represents what is most important in shopping malls, including organizing stores in clusters for the benefit of customers and improving sales, supported by statistical experiments showing consistency and expected behavior.

Thanks to implementing the simulator with an architecture based on a multi-agent system with emotional BDI agents, it is possible to simulate customers' behavior with great precision, including the possible specializations or generalizations of the agents achieving the objectives proposed in this work.

Acknowledgements. The author Jairo Enrique Serrano Castañeda thanks MinCiencias, the Pontificia Universidad Javeriana and the Universidad Tecnológica de Bolívar for the support received to pursue a doctoral degree within "Becas de la Excelencia Doctoral del Bicentenario (corte 1)".

References

1. Adam, C., Gaudou, B.: BDI agents in social simulations: a survey. Knowl. Eng. Rev. **31**(3), 207–238 (2016). https://doi.org/10.1017/S0269888916000096
2. Ali, W., Moulin, B.: 2D-3D MultiAgent GeoSimulation with Knowledge-Based Agents of Customers' Shopping Behavior in a Shopping Mall. In: Cohn, A.G., Mark, D.M. (eds.) COSIT 2005. LNCS, vol. 3693, pp. 445–458. Springer, Heidelberg (2005). https://doi.org/10.1007/11556114_28
3. Andres Armando de la Peña: RoboAct modelo de control autónomo y cooperativo para el Teatro Robótico. Ph.D. thesis, Pontificia Universidad Javeriana (2014)
4. Angel, R., Gonzalez, E.: Agent-based social simulation: General requirements and for a Colombian approach. In: 2012 7th Colombian Computing Congress (CCC). pp. 1–6. IEEE (10 2012). https://doi.org/10.1109/ColombianCC.2012.6398033
5. Boero, R., Bravo, G., Castellani, M., Squazzoni, F.: Why bother with what others tell you? An experimental data-driven agent-based model. JASSS **13**(3) (2010). https://doi.org/10.18564/jasss.1620, http://jasss.soc.surrey.ac.uk/13/3/6.html
6. Bratman, M.E., Israel, D.J., Pollack, M.E.: Plans and resource-bounded practical reasoning. Comput. Intell. **4**(3), 349–355 (9 1988). https://doi.org/10.1111/j.1467-8640.1988.tb00284.x
7. Bray, J.P.: Consumer behaviour theory: approaches and models. pp. 1–33 (2008), http://eprints.bournemouth.ac.uk/10107/4/licence.txt
8. Burke, R.R., Leykin, A.: Identifying the drivers of shopper attention, engagement, and purchase. In: The Routledge Companion to Marketing Research, pp. 319–355. Routledge, New York : Routledge, 2021. — Series: Routledge companions in business, management and accounting (2021). https://doi.org/10.4324/9781315544892-21

9. Copley, P.: For the love of AIDA - developing the Hierarchy of Effects model in SME social media marketing strategy. ISBE Conference, pp. 1–15 (2015)
10. González, E., Avila, J., Bustacara, C.: BESA: Behavior-Oriented Social-Based Agent Framework. undefined, Event-Driven (2003)
11. Han, F., Liu, L., Zhang, Y.: Pathfinder-based simulation and optimisation of personnel evacuation modelling of a shopping mall. J. Phys.: Conf. Ser. **1757**(1), 012112 (2021). https://doi.org/10.1088/1742-6596/1757/1/012112
12. Hu, J., Guan, C.: A model of emotional agent based on granular computing. In: 2011 Seventh International Conference on Computational Intelligence and Security. pp. 190–194. IEEE (2011). https://doi.org/10.1109/CIS.2011.50
13. Lisotto, M., Coscia, P., Ballan, L.: Social and scene-aware trajectory prediction in crowded spaces. In: 2019 IEEE/CVF International Conference on Computer Vision Workshop (ICCVW). pp. 2567–2574. IEEE (2019). https://doi.org/10.1109/ICCVW.2019.00314
14. Luneski, A., Moore, R.K.: Affective computing and collaborative networks: towards emotion-aware interaction. In: Pervasive Collaborative Networks, vol. 283, pp. 315–322. Springer, US, Boston, MA (2008). https://doi.org/10.1007/978-0-387-84837-2_32
15. MacDowell, K.A., Mandler, G.: Constructions of emotion: discrepancy, arousal, and mood. Motiv. Emot. **13**(2), 105–124 (1989). https://doi.org/10.1007/BF00992957
16. Moga, H., Sandu, F., Danciu, G.M., Boboc, R., Constantinescu, I.: Extended control-value emotional agent based on fuzzy logic approach. In: 2013 11th RoEduNet International Conference. pp. 1–8. IEEE (1 2013). https://doi.org/10.1109/RoEduNet.2013.6511734
17. Ortony, A., Clore, G.L., Collins, A.: The Cognitive Structure of Emotions. Cambridge University Press (7 1988). https://doi.org/10.1017/CBO9780511571299
18. Rodríguez, J., Torres, M., González, E.: LA METODOLOGÍA AOPOA. Avances en Sistemas e Informática 4(2) (5 2007)
19. Roux, G.: Quenches in quantum many-body systems: One-dimensional Bose-Hubbard model reexamined. 4th Workshop on Emotion and Computing pp. 1–8 (10 2008). https://doi.org/10.1103/PhysRevA.79.021608
20. Shannon, R.E.: Simulation: a survey with research suggestions. A I I E Trans. **7**(3), 289–301 (1975). https://doi.org/10.1080/05695557508975010
21. Silverman, E.: Analysis: Frameworks and theories for social simulation. In: Methodological Investigations in Agent-Based Modelling, pp. 107–123. Springer International Publishing, Cham (2018). https://doi.org/10.1007/978-3-319-72408-9_6
22. Squazzoni, F., Jager, W., Edmonds, B.: Social simulation in the social sciences. Soc. Sci. Comput. Rev. **32**(3), 279–294 (2014). https://doi.org/10.1177/0894439313512975

Classification of Depression Based on Audio with Artificial Intelligence

Ana M. López-Echeverry⊕, Sebastián López-Flórez(✉)⊕,
and Jovanny Bedoya Guapacha⊕

Universidad Tecnológica de Pereira, Cra. 27 10-02, Pereira, Risaralda, Colombia
{anamayi,sebastianlopezflorez,jovan}@utp.edu.co

Abstract. In this article, we propose a model for the recognition of depression based on a 1D convolutional neural network and preprocessing that allows the extraction of relevant information from the audio generated by patients from a diagnostic interview based on the PHQ-8 questionnaire. The experiments were carried out with the data set provided by the Audio-Visual Emotion Challenge (AVEC 2016), a resampling strategy and a low-pass filter are introduced during the training phase of the model to eliminate background noise and to balance the positive and negative samples, avoiding the bias that generates the uneven distribution of the sample. The experimental results achieved, clearly demonstrate the effectiveness of the proposed approach.

Keywords: Depression recognition · Audio representation · CNN · Deep learning

1 Introduction

According to WHO (World Health Organization) studies, depression is a mental disorder that occurs commonly among human beings, reporting prevalence range between 15 to 25%, this being a dynamic state that a person expresses in everyday life through behaviours and interactions that allow individual and collective subjects to deploy their resources emotional, cognitive and mental [18,23]. Concepts of depressive disorder consider perspectives involving not only medical conditions but also cultural partner and behavioural aspects. From the cognitive-behavioural approach, Beck (1972) defines depression as a series of negative thoughts about yourself, the world, and the future; that generates a series of systematic distortions in the processing of information that creates conditions of anguish, sadness, anxiety and defenselessness. Stating that the typical emotions and behaviour of depression are usually determined by how the depressive perceives reality [35]. According to WHO [9,27], although there are effective treatments for depression, sometimes it is not considered relevant to public health, which means that more than half of those affected worldwide do not receive adequate treatment. Being one of the main obstacles erroneous clinical evaluation due to a large amount of information to be processed by the treating physician

© Springer Nature Switzerland AG 2022
E. Gonzalez et al. (Eds.): CCC 2021, CCIS 1594, pp. 19–30, 2022.
https://doi.org/10.1007/978-3-031-19951-6_2

in psychological and behavioural terms, also considering that current diagnoses are mainly subjective, presenting inconsistencies between treating professionals, which leads to reprocesses that imply higher professional care costs for people requiring treatment [27]. Additionally, the first signs of depression are difficult to detect and quantify since these are strongly affected by subjective observation from clinicians. Besides there is a lack of a long-term follow-up diagnosis [23]. As the number of patients with depression increases, an extra burden is placed on physicians who prevents the accurate diagnosis of clinical depression [16]. Understanding that suicide is an indirect result of the presence of states of major depression in individuals, the WHO suggests, based on scientific evidence, that a national suicide strategy must have four fundamental elements [19].

1. Restriction of access to resources (such as weapons) to commit suicide.
2. Strengthen educational programs for the young population by providing tools to solve problems and develop life skills.
3. Early identification of individuals who are at risk of suicide (or who have tried to commit suicide), and transversal contact with them.
4. Interaction with the media (the press) to promote responsible coverage of suicide and mental health issues.

Additionally, the recommendations established by the WHO include diagnosis and treatment of mental illnesses, being necessary the estimation of depression in well-defined conditions and strictly comparable, there are diagnostic instruments based on questionnaires clinical depression standards that provide clear guidance for treating clinicians in relation to different risk conditions that can be evaluated through the guiding questions, thus allowing to establish the presence or not of depression [19,24].

Taking into account the difficulties that arise in the process of diagnosis of depression, it is necessary to develop a solution that allows the detection of the disease in a reliable and accessible way, complying with the established by the WHO linking the diagnostic questionnaires in addition to new technologies that allow the inclusion of behavioural characteristics extracted from audio [4], Therefore, techniques for the identification of features associated with depression from audio.

Current studies on screening for depression use interviews with the Wizard of Oz from Distress Analysis Interview Corpus (DAIC) Wizard-of-Oz (WOZ) to study depression among adults. The authors in [30] propose a framework for the recognition of depression through a bimodal analysis composed of a deep convolutional neural network (DCNN) and a deep neural network (DNN) model from audio and video. In addition, the authors in [26] propose the automatic use of primitives of human behaviour detecting facial markers as series of time of low-dimensional multichannel. Those primitives are used to create two description cycles that allow the calculus of statistics at the sequence level of behavioural primitives and, the second cycle poses the problem as a convolutional neural network operating on a spectral representation of multichannel behavioural signals. Additionally, the authors in [32] propose deep and also superficial models for the estimation and classification of depression from audio, video and text descriptors with a hybrid framework consisting of three main parts: 1) A recognition model of audiovisual multimodal depression based on a DCNN and a DNN to estimate the scale of depression of the patient health questionnaire (PHQ-8); 2) A model based on Paragraph Vector (PV) and Support Vector Machine (SVM) to infer the physical and mental conditions of the individual from the transcripts of the interview; 3) A random forest (RF) model for classification depression from esti-mated PHQ-8 score and conditions inferred from the individual. We consider a preprocessing stage that increases the sample set resulting in an improvement of the prediction performance. The model is built based on a convolutional network 1D. Using as input a 15-second segment of audio that is processed through the library specialized in audio processing. The main contributions of this work are summarized below:

1. We study the effect of the behaviour of the normalized data, increasing the information in batches based on the precision of the detection, and then we design the best network from the results of the experimental tests.
2. We propose a simple but effective depression detection method based on end-to-end 1D CNN architecture to classify time series 1D audio signals directly without converting them to 2D data. Through a thorough evaluation, we demonstrate that our method achieves equivalent results to what is pre-sented by the compared methods reducing the complexity of the network significantly.

The rest of this document is organized as follows. Section 3 first provides an overview of the proposed method, describes the data preprocessing algorithm, and then the design of 1D CNN. In Sect. 4, we show the numerical analysis and performance comparison. Finally, in Sect. 5, we conclude.

2   Related Work

In recent years, research on mental health aspects has been getting stronger as large volumes of data of a different typology that were initially used in the detection of emotions and have transcended to support studies that validate their application in screening for mental illness. Deep learning algorithms most used since 2017 as neural networks have been used in a variety of processes focused on generating solutions from the treatment of audio, video and image signals. In particular, there have been studies that allow identifying the existence of clin-ical depression and its degree of classification [26,30,32]. These investigations have been carried out on public data sets available through competitions such as AVEC 2016 and its other versions. These focus primarily on the identifica-tion of emotions from the analysis of facial expressions and voice prosody, in addition, in some cases, the inclusion of the decomposition of the characteristics of the text. Data generated from Eyepieces movements and electroencephalo-grams EEG have also been widely used for the detection of depression for the advantages concerning being considered non-invasive for people [34]. However, the equipment required to obtain these signals is highly specialized and expensive. The authors have found that the subjects depressed are prone to have a low dynamic range of the fundamental frequency, slow speech rate, slightly shorter speech duration, and relatively monotonous delivery [1,5,29,32], the authors in [33] investigated the relationship between the severity of depression and vocal prosodies, such as pause change and fundamental vocal frequency. Based on this, is possible to consider the evaluation of depression by means of analysis audio. In related work, Jain et al. [13], combined visual functions LBP-TOP with dense paths and bass audio descriptors level provided in [28]. The audiovisual characteristics extracted were encoded using a Fisher linear vector representation [8].

The authors in [26] indicate that the human behaviour shown in the videos and described in terms of primitive behaviours can provide information relevant to the analysis of depression. For the analysis of depression, the authors in [27] conducted three experiments to examine the usefulness of non-verbal characteristics for detecting depression. They adopted two video-based methods (FACS encoding and face tracking based on AAM) and an audio method to evaluate the vocal expression. In other research, good performance has been achieved in depression detection studies using low-level descriptors (LLD), such as quality voice, prosody characteristics, spectral descriptors and their high-level statistical functions [6,11,21,31]. Additionally, the authors in [2,17] consider as problematic working with these characteristics, due to the theoretical foundation required, the difficulty of generalizing the databases and the increased computational time needed for the analysis. On the other hand, the statistical methods summarize the low-level characteristics and, even though this summary may introduce a loss of information, these methods overcome these deficiencies at the moment to make a decision. At present in the field of computer vision, the basic characteristics are extracted by means of previously trained deep learning networks, such as AlexNet, Visual Geometry Group VGG and ResNet. This has allowed some researchers to generate models with better performance in detecting depression [3,14,20]. Based on the analysis presented in the state of the art, this research proposes a system that includes a pre-processing stage that allows adapting the data to consolidate a training set where classes with the same number of samples are held, avoiding biases in the results. Additionally, we eliminate the stages of audio transformation to spectrograms and image processing, allowing using a lightweight system with the same performance and less computational demand.

In general, people who suffer from clinical depression are reluctant or unable to carry out activities on a daily basis, generating problems at the family, work or school level. Therefore, priority should be given to intervention by increasing the capacities of basic service professionals for the diagnosis, treatment and remission of the most prevalent mental disorders, with an emphasis on childhood and adolescence, in such a way as to reduce depression in university students who present a level of depression higher by 30.6%, like other population groups that suffer from the disease, additionally, an intelligent rapid response system for clinical depression disorder would allow to diagnose and closely monitor the long-term symptomatology. For this, there are various mechanisms, such as clinical interviews and simple questionnaires, among which are the Beck Depression Inventory - BDI, Center for Epidemiologic Studies Depression Scale, Geriatric Depression Scale, Hospital Anxiety and Depression Scale, Edinburgh Postnatal D and in particular the Patient Health Questionary PHQ-8 questionnaire will be used.

3   Methodology

Considering the advantages of convolutional neural networks applied to the processing of audio signals compared to methods of machine-learning analysis, this article presents a model based on a 1D convolutional neural network for extraction of speech characteristics related to depression to identify patients with this condition. Figure 1 shows the methodological development carried out during the model implementation, including a general scheme.

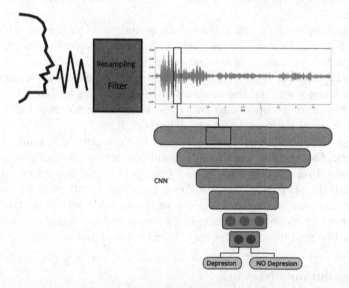

Fig. 1. Feature diagram

3.1   Pre-processing

Before bringing the audio samples into the network, we process them to make them fit. Additionally, to guarantee that we use the audio sample from the patient, we use the information associated with the analysis of the textual intervention during the interview performed using the PHQ-8 questionnaire, to identify the times in which the patient intervenes, making it possible to extract the signal fragments from the sample, which then are concatenated to have a continuous signal over time. Subsequently, we performed a 15-second segmentation from the 60-second signal.

3.2 Database

In this project, we use the AVEC 2016 database, which contains clinics interviews to support the diagnosis of psychological distress and conditions such as anxiety, depression, and post-traumatic stress disorder [10]. The data-set consists of three subsets of samples resulting from interviews, face to face, through the Wizard of Oz system with a virtual interviewer named Ellie, and through the SimSensei system controlled by artificial intelligence. With a total of 351 participants, of which 120 were face to face, 86 men and 34 women, 140 participants from the Wizard of Oz, 76 men, 63 women and, one who did not answer about their gender and 91 from the SimSensei system, 55 men, 35 women and one did not report their gender [7]. Teleconference and face-to-face interviews took between 30 and 60 min., the Wizard of Oz from 5 to 20 min. and automated interviews 15–25 min. [10].

The database contains 92 GB of data stored as a package of 189 folders compressed in zip format. In the folder, each file represents a single session containing a text transcript of the recording, the audio files of the participants, and the facial features. The level of depression was labelled with a single value per record using a standardized self-rated subjective depression scale, PHQ-8 [22]. The files were grouped into two folders according to their PHQ-8 score, classifying them as depressed and not depressed.

Through the library and the Digital signal Processing [25] guide for audio management, the following treatment was carried out on the audio samples, files were cut into 15-s samples from the second 60 to avoid noise from the background, with the purpose of capturing enough sentences allowing the identification of relevant characteristics of speech in the training set. Next, the samples were increased by means of a resampling process and the signal was purified by means of a low-pass filter to subsequently enter the signal into the 1D network.

3.3 Convolutional Network

The proposed architecture contains five (5) convolutional blocks, six (6) fully connected layers and a Softmax layer as an output prediction, as shown in Fig. 2. The convolutional block consists of a convolutional layer, a rectified linear unit (ReLU) layer and, a max-pooling layer. We add a batch normalization layer (BN) [12] after the ReLU activation only in the first convolutional block to normalize the input layer, adjusting and scaling the activations. The bach normalization BN normalizes the input to the zero mean and unit variance, which improves the performance and stability of the deep neural network [15]. Then, we introduce two (2) convolutional blocks that share the same structure. In the last stage of processing, we use the six (6) completely connected layers, plus an abandonment layer and a Softmax output that generates the decision in terms of a probability for depressive and non-depressive.

Figure 2. shows the architecture of the 1D convolutional network used for the detection of depression from audio. Once the network was implemented and trained, we carried out the validation process and finally, we used the test data set provided by the AVEC competence for the testing process.

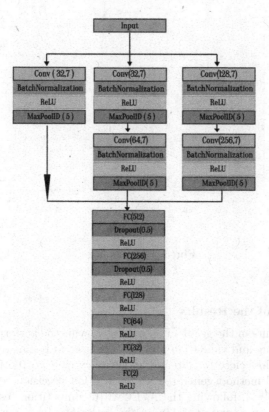

Fig. 2. 1D-CNN architecture

4   Results

We perform all the experiments using a PC available in the laboratory with a graphics card Nvidia GTX 2060 and an Intel I7 processor of the ninth generation. Additionally, we use the Jupyter Notebook application, allowing access to compare the code and results with other researchers.

For the construction of the convolutional 1D network, we use the Tensor Flow library. We evaluate the results of our ranking using four metrics [31] accuracy, precision, sensitivity and measurement F1. We prepared the 1D convolutional network and included the training data and test, performing a network-tuning process according to the data output, allowing us to obtain results comparable with the authors in [4]. We completed the filtering and normalization of the audio signal using the butter lowpass filter and Z Score for normalization.

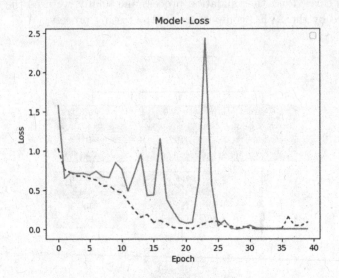

Fig. 3. Function loss

4.1   Analysis of the Results

We show the results in the graphs Fig. 4 y Fig. 3, whit the performance obtained during the training and validation process. The system begins to converge from epoch 25 with a loss close to zero and an accuracy close to 100%.

The proposed method generated a classification precision result of 0.602 ± 0.046% (See Table 1), following the AVEC 2016 competition test and test protocol, generating an accuracy of 43% in the detection of non-depressed patients and 73% in patients with depression with the test set used in the competition, these data being totally new for the trained network. Unlike what is presented by the authors in [4] where they used a smaller set with 27 samples for which 20 normal patients and one depressed were correctly classified, taking into account that 6 samples of a total of 7 depressed were classified incorrectly, generating a failure of 85.7% in the detection of depression. In our implementation, we used 47 samples of depressed people for training, as observed in the confusion matrix Fig. 5, with a success rate 0.73 for depressed patients and 23% false negatives.

5   Conclusion

We achieved the classification of depression from the prosody of the voice through the implementation of a deep neural network. We capture relevant information

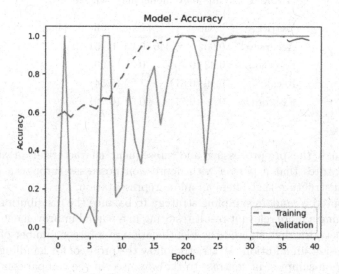

Fig. 4. Function accuracy

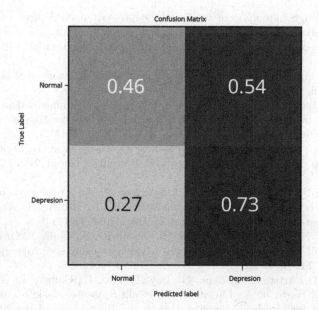

Fig. 5. The confusion matrix for the DAIC-WOZ database validation scenario is shown following the specifications of the test audios proposed by the challenge. This configuration achieves an overall accuracy of $0.602 \pm 0.046\%$, matching the state of the art with an architecture with less processing requirements. The ideal model (trained in all available publications) achieves a precision 61%

Table 1. Results base model and own model

Metrics	Own	DeepAudionet [4]
Accuracy %	0.602 ± 0.046	0.65 (0.65)
Precision %	0.43 (0.79)	0.35 (1.00)
Recall %	0.59 (0.67)	1.00 (0.54)
F1-score %	0.56 (0.77)	0.52 (0.70)

going through the pre-processing and subsequent characterization about the intrinsic features that a person with depression possesses through a 1D CNN hierarchical structure that offers an audio representation.

We adopted a random sampling strategy to balance the distribution uneven, thus obtaining a more relevant result resulting in a partial improvement based on a simpler network that allowed the identification of a larger number of patients with depression. In addition, we strictly follow the protocol for handling training and validation samples, in contrast to the way used in the comparison research.

References

1. Alghowinem, S.: From joyous to clinically depressed: mood detection using multi-modal analysis of a person's appearance and speech. In: 2013 Humaine Association Conference on Affective Computing and Intelligent Interaction. pp. 648–654. IEEE (2013)
2. Alghowinem, S. et al.: Multimodal analysis of verbal and nonverbal behaviour on the example of clinical depression (2015)
3. Chao, L., Tao, J., Yang, M., Li, Y.: Multi task sequence learning for depression scale prediction from video. In: 2015 International Conference on Affective Computing and Intelligent Interaction (ACII). pp. 526–531. IEEE (2015)
4. Chlasta, K., Wołk, K., Krejtz, I.: Automated speech-based screening of depression using deep convolutional neural networks. Procedia Comput. Sci. **164**, 618–628 (2019)
5. Cummins, N., Epps, J., Breakspear, M., Goecke, R.: An investigation of depressed speech detection: Features and normalization. In: Twelfth Annual Conference of the International Speech Communication Association (2011)
6. Cummins, N., Scherer, S., Krajewski, J., Schnieder, S., Epps, J., Quatieri, T.F.: A review of depression and suicide risk assessment using speech analysis. Speech Commun. **71**, 10–49 (2015)
7. DeVault, D., Artstein, R., Benn, G., Dey, T., Fast, E., Gainer, A., Georgila, K., Gratch, J., Hartholt, A., Lhommet, M., et al.: Simsensei kiosk: a virtual human interviewer for healthcare decision support. In: Proceedings of the 2014 International Conference on Autonomous Agents and Multi-agent Systems. pp. 1061–1068 (2014)
8. Dibeklioğlu, H., Hammal, Z., Cohn, J.F.: Dynamic multimodal measurement of depression severity using deep autoencoding. IEEE J. Biomed. Health Inform. **22**(2), 525–536 (2017)

9. Evans-Lacko, S., Aguilar-Gaxiola, S., Al-Hamzawi, A., Alonso, J., Benjet, C., Bruf-faerts, R., Chiu, W., Florescu, S., de Girolamo, G., Gureje, O., et al.: Socio-economic variations in the mental health treatment gap for people with anxiety, mood, and substance use disorders: results from the who world mental health (wmh) surveys. Psychol. Med. **48**(9), 1560–1571 (2018)

10. Gratch, J., Artstein, R., Lucas, G., Stratou, G., Scherer, S., Nazarian, A., Wood, R., Boberg, J., DeVault, D., Marsella, S., et al.: The distress analysis interview corpus of human and computer interviews. In: Proceedings of the Ninth International Conference on Language Resources and Evaluation (LREC'14). pp. 3123–3128 (2014)

11. He, L., Jiang, D., Sahli, H.: Multimodal depression recognition with dynamic visual and audio cues. In: 2015 International Conference on Affective Computing and Intelligent Interaction (ACII). pp. 260–266. IEEE (2015)

12. Ioffe, S., Szegedy, C.: Batch normalization: accelerating deep network training by reducing internal covariate shift. In: International Conference on Machine Learning. pp. 448–456. PMLR (2015)

13. Jain, V., Crowley, J.L., Dey, A.K., Lux, A.: Depression estimation using audiovisual features and fisher vector encoding. In: Proceedings of the 4th International Workshop on Audio/Visual Emotion Challenge. pp. 87–91 (2014)

14. Jan, A., Meng, H., Gaus, Y.F.B.A., Zhang, F.: Artificial intelligent system for automatic depression level analysis through visual and vocal expressions. IEEE Trans. Cognit. Dev. Syst. **10**(3), 668–680 (2017)

15. LeCun, Y., Bengio, Y., Hinton, G.: Deep learning. Nature **521**(7553), 436–444 (2015)

16. Li, J., Fu, X., Shao, Z., Shang, Y.: Improvement on speech depression recognition based on deep networks. In: 2018 Chinese Automation Congress (CAC). pp. 2705–2709. IEEE (2018)

17. Morales, M.R.: Multimodal depression detection: an investigation of features and fusion techniques for automated systems. City University of New York (2018)

18. Olmedo-Buenrostro, B.A., Jorge, T.H., Velasco-Rodríguez, R., Mora-Brambila, A.B., Azucena, B.V.L.: Prevalencia y severidad de depresión en estudiantes de enfermería de la universidad de colima. Revista de Enfermería del Instituto Mexicano del Seguro Social **14**(1), 17–22 (2006)

19. Organization, W.H., et al.: WHO European framework for action on mental health 2021–2025 (2022)

20. Pampouchidou, A., Pediaditis, M., Maridaki, A., Awais, M., Vazakopoulou, C.-M., Sfakianakis, S., Tsiknakis, M., Simos, P., Marias, K., Yang, F., Meriaudeau, F.: Quantitative comparison of motion history image variants for video-based depression assessment. EURASIP J. Image Video Process. **2017**(1), 1–11 (2017). https://doi.org/10.1186/s13640-017-0212-3

21. Pampouchidou, A., Simantiraki, O., Fazlollahi, A., Pediaditis, M., Manousos, D., Roniotis, A., Giannakakis, G., Meriaudeau, F., Simos, P., Marias, K., et al.: Depression assessment by fusing high and low level features from audio, video, and text. In: Proceedings of the 6th International Workshop on Audio/Visual Emotion Challenge. pp. 27–34 (2016)

22. Ringeval, F., Schuller, B., Valstar, M., Gratch, J., Cowie, R., Scherer, S., Mozgai, S., Cummins, N., Schmitt, M., Pantic, M.: Avec 2017: Real-life depression, and affect recognition workshop and challenge. In: Proceedings of the 7th Annual Workshop on Audio/Visual Emotion Challenge. pp. 3–9 (2017)

23. de Enfermedades No Transmisibles Grupo Funcional: Gestión Integrada para la Salud Mental, S.: Actualización Guía Metodológica para el Observatorio Nacional de Salud mental. Imprenta Nacional de Colombia, Ministerio de Salud y Protección Social, 1rd edn. (Bogotá, Enero de 2017)

24. Simon, G.E., Rutter, C.M., Peterson, D., Oliver, M., Whiteside, U., Operskalski, B., Ludman, E.J.: Does response on the PHQ-9 depression questionnaire predict subsequent suicide attempt or suicide death? Psychiatr. Serv. **64**(12), 1195–1202 (2013)

25. Smith, S.: Digital Signal Processing: A Practical Guide for Engineers and Scientists. Elsevier (2013)

26. Song, S., Shen, L., Valstar, M.: Human behaviour-based automatic depression analysis using hand-crafted statistics and deep learned spectral features. In: 2018 13th IEEE International Conference on Automatic Face & Gesture Recognition (FG 2018). pp. 158–165. IEEE (2018)

27. Valladares Guamán, J.N.: Depresión y rendimiento académico en estudiantes de segundo año de bachillerato de una institución educativa, santo domingo, ecuador 2021 (2022)

28. Valstar, M., Schuller, B., Smith, K., Almaev, T., Eyben, F., Krajewski, J., Cowie, R., Pantic, M.: Avec 2014: 3D dimensional affect and depression recognition challenge. In: Proceedings of the 4th International Workshop On Audio/visual Emotion Challenge. pp. 3–10 (2014)

29. Williamson, J.R., Quatieri, T.F., Helfer, B.S., Horwitz, R., Yu, B., Mehta, D.D.: Vocal biomarkers of depression based on motor incoordination. In: Proceedings of the 3rd ACM International Workshop on Audio/Visual Emotion Challenge. pp. 41–48 (2013)

30. Yang, L., Jiang, D., Han, W., Sahli, H.: DCNN and DNN based multi-modal depression recognition. In: 2017 Seventh International Conference on Affective Computing and Intelligent Interaction (ACII). pp. 484–489. IEEE (2017)

31. Yang, L., Jiang, D., He, L., Pei, E., Oveneke, M.C., Sahli, H.: Decision tree based depression classification from audio video and language information. In: Proceedings of the 6th International Workshop on Audio/Visual Emotion Challenge. pp. 89–96 (2016)

32. Yang, L., Jiang, D., Sahli, H.: Integrating deep and shallow models for multi-modal depression analysis-hybrid architectures. IEEE Trans. Affect. Comput. **12**(1), 239–253 (2018)

33. Yang, Y., Fairbairn, C., Cohn, J.F.: Detecting depression severity from vocal prosody. IEEE Trans. Affect. Comput. **4**(2), 142–150 (2012)

34. Zhu, J., Wang, Z., Gong, T., Zeng, S., Li, X., Hu, B., Li, J., Sun, S., Zhang, L.: An improved classification model for depression detection using EEG and eye tracking data. IEEE Trans. Nanobiosci. **19**(3), 527–537 (2020)

35. Zúñiga, M.Á., Jacobo, B.R., Rodríguez, A.S., Cabrera, N.C., Rentería, M.L.J.: La relación entre depresión y conflictos familiares en adolescentes. Int. J. Psychol. Psychol. Ther. **9**(2), 205–216 (2009)

Analytical Model of Recommendations for the Mitigation of Theft Risks

Juan Camilo Montaña🆔 and Enrique Gonzalez(✉)🆔

Pontificia Universidad Javeriana, Bogota, D.C, Colombia
{juanc_montana,egonzal}@javeriana.edu.co

Abstract. Crime rates around the world are constantly increasing, and the crime of theft is one of those that most affects the population. This type of crime has occurrences and patterns in certain places and periods. This article presents an analytical model that allows generating recommendations to mitigate the risk of being a victim of this crime. The model is responsible for preprocessing the data, performing fuzzy partitioning, generating frequent patterns, and creating fuzzy association rules to generate recommendations. The model was applied to the case study associated with the area with the highest theft crimes rate in Bogotá.

Keywords: Recommendations model · Fuzzy partitioning · Theft risk · Association rules

1 Introduction

Currently, there are different studies aimed at predicting, studying, and/or analyzing the behavior of crime through the application of *artificial intelligence (AI)* techniques. Often, the goal is to decrease the crime rate by identifying crime areas based on crime category and protecting criminal areas. Crimes are influenced by criminal organizations and have a high dependence on the characteristics of the places where they occur frequently. The main utility of analyzing crime areas is to identify the areas of greatest danger after analyzing clusters and frequent crime occurrences over different years, based on structured data collected by law enforcement authorities or other organizations. Crime prediction is used to identify and characterize the areas in which crimes are committed and to take preventive actions to decrease the crime rate.

In recent years, the theft to people has become one of the greatest public policy challenges for citizen security. In particular, according to the survey of coexistence and citizen security in 2019 [1], in 2018, 8.6% of the people surveyed in municipal capitals were victims of this crime in Colombia. Even in some cities, such as Bogotá, Pasto, or Villavicencio, more than 10% of respondents reported having a personal item stolen from them in the previous year.

Theft is a type of crime against common property around the world, which generally refers to the act of illegal possession of private or public property. In recent years, despite of the generally falling crime rates, preventing, and combating crime remains a challenge. Local governments and police departments often pay more attention to murder, assault,

© Springer Nature Switzerland AG 2022
E. Gonzalez et al. (Eds.): CCC 2021, CCIS 1594, pp. 31–45, 2022.
https://doi.org/10.1007/978-3-031-19951-6_3

and other violent crimes [2], thus limited resources are allocated to prevent or combat crime against property. Therefore, the rate of robbery crimes seems much higher than that of violent crimes. In addition, effective prevention strategies against new types of theft (such as electric vehicle theft) are quite inadequate. Quantitative and accurate risk analysis is vital to prevent theft when police resources are limited. Furthermore, there are strong correlations between crime rates and other variables such as the geographic location of a community, the day of the week, and the time of year (seasonal patterns) [3].

Crime data allows organizations and ordinary citizens to obtain information related to the safety of their environment. Crime forecasting is related to predicting a crime before it occurs. Currently, police use tools to assist in specific tasks, such as listening to a suspect's phone call or using a body camera to record some unusual illegal activity [4].

In this context, this paper presents the *RMFAR (Recommender Model with Fuzzy Association Rules)* recommendation model based on WFAR *(Weighted Fuzzy Association Rules)*. This model is designed to generate recommendations that allow citizens to mitigate the risk of being victims of theft crimes. The proposed model, unlike most of the previous proposed works, uses a solid base of information that integrates different data sources to reduce the problem of data shortages. In addition, in terms of association rules, it groups the data and uses a more powerful algorithm such as *FP-Growth (Frequent Pattern Growth)* to obtain better rules. In order to achieve a better understanding from the system users, the fuzzy association rules use a terminology more oriented to the real world and easier to understand by the citizens. Finally, the approach used to generate recommendations is different from that of most of these types of systems; small variations are made on the rules closest to the users' queries in order to identify and evaluate better alternatives that serve as useful recommendations for citizens.

This paper starts by presenting the state of the art for the review of previous works and the consolidation process of data for the construction of an extended database. Subsequently, the fuzzy association rules and the recommendations model are introduced. Finally, the evaluation, experimentation results, and conclusions are discussed.

2 Related Work

In the context of Colombia, Gimenez proposed a study using *RTM (Risk Terrain Modeling)* [5] to identify which places have a higher or lower risk of victimization from violent crimes. Thus, to produce actionable information to improve public security in Bogotá, this study offers a comprehensive account of the main environmental factors of vulnerability and exposure to crime. Cobos et al. [6] presented a machine learning model, based on support vector machines for regression *(SRV)*, adjusted for the prediction of the trend of thefts in Colombia. Gelvez et al. [7] used a signal processing model for graphs and an adaptation of the TF-IDF text vectorization model applied to the temporal space case; this work found that the best results for crime prediction were given when using the models with spatial relationships of graphs per week. According to Gimenez, a prediction model only presents a diagnosis and then the authorities must take care of finding the cure [5]. The vast majority of authors present their studies as an analysis that serves as the basis for later use by other individuals to prevent crimes, usually local authorities. Therefore, the lack of a citizen-oriented prevention approach is evident.

A common problem in current crime prediction methods is that, given detailed spatial-temporal units, crime data would become very scarce, and prediction would not work properly. However, by modeling crime prediction as a recommendation problem, one can make use of the abundant selection of methods in recommendation systems that inherently consider the scarcity of data. Zhang et al. [8] proposed modeling crime prediction as a recommendation problem. By using this kind of modeling, you can have finer spatial-temporal granularity by using techniques in recommendation systems to mitigate the problem of data scarcity. In this work, the method for modeling spatial and temporal factors as users and elements was presented, and it discussed several recommendation techniques that can be applied. These techniques include collaborative filtering methods as well as context-based rating prediction methods. This recommendation system was only used as a prediction method and not to make recommendations. The scarcity of data is higher because the authors only use data related to time (date and time) and space (latitude and longitude); for this reason, the opportunity arises to have a more solid database to obtain much more complete results.

From the perspective of data mining, another approach is to find patterns in crime data, such as the one presented by Zhang et al., where the authors use fuzzy logic to establish a high, medium, or low crime rate to later generate frequent patterns using the *FP-Growth* algorithm, and fuzzy association rules. As a result, there are many interesting and surprising rules, which deserve to be studied further by domain experts. A similar analysis was presented by Englin in [9]; this work extracted meaningful relationships from unclean public data by employing indirect association rules over the available attributes. This paper also concludes that mining of indirect association rules for crime data has the potential to provide interesting relationships between data but requires more manipulation of data and rules. In addition, another conclusion, from this data, is that it would have been interesting to extend the algorithm and clean the dataset to create a set that has attributes with a reduced number of possible values, thus allowing the production of more potential rules. When grouping common crime descriptors or location descriptors, the support for these values would have been greater, which would have resulted in more rules with more of those attributes [9].

Considering the existing work, it is identified as an aspect to consider the limitation of the data of the study area to a city so that the information is more consistent and specialized. In general, most works present a diagnosis and analysis so that later the police authorities can use them to act. In contrast, this work contributes to a citizen-oriented approach. In addition, often non-significant details are reported, which means that the work cannot be used as a point of comparison or be reproducible.

The terminology is very specialized at the scientific level, so it becomes difficult to understand and interpret by ordinary citizens. Another contribution of this work is to use fuzzy logic to create rules of association closer to the natural language that can be understood and interpretable by citizens. Many of the previous works only use basic location information. Moreover, the present work built a solid database by consolidating various databases and integrating new information from sources such as Google Maps, an approach that no other previous work has taken. Regarding the rules of the association, improvements were raised by Englin in [9] which proposes to carry out a grouping of the data to generate more powerful rules of the association. In the present work, the grouping of some data is carried out, and additionally, the data is grouped using fuzzy sets.

Besides, this model uses an algorithm that is more efficient at generating association rules and that does not slow down the number of records. Another novelty of this work is that it uses the FP-Growth algorithm, which has many advantages over the A priori algorithm, that will be referenced later. Finally, the recommendation system proposed in this domain is used to make predictions or classifications. In the model presented in this paper, an inverse recommendation is used; that is, based on some input data from the user, a variation is made on this data to identify if there is a rule that minimizes the feasibility of theft risk.

3 Data Consolidation

The case study for this work is the crimes of theft committed in the area of Suba in Bogotá during the year 2020. This area has the highest number of theft crimes in the city. It has 14.3% of the city's population and the largest socioeconomic diversity, ranging from stratum 1 to 5. To overcome the limitations of previous work, in particular those related to data scarcity, a consolidated database was built by integrating different data sources and creating new key variables from existing open data.

3.1 Exploring the Data

Different data sources were used for building the consolidated database, such as:

1. *Statistical, Criminal, Contraventional, and Operational Information System of the National Police (SIEDCO), of the Directorate of Criminal Investigation and Interpol (DIJIN)*: contains the information on theft crimes for the year 2020 corresponding to the neighborhoods of the area of Suba.[1]
2. *Special Administrative Unit of District Cadastre (UAECD):* contains the information of the cadastral sectors of Suba.[2]
3. *District Secretary for Women (SDM):* contains information on the UPZ of Suba and night safety indices for each of them.[3]

Interviews with crime experts allowed identifying the main variables to be taken into account. Besides place, time, victim, and offender variables, other ones related to the factors that are considered the most influential for the analysis of a theft crime were identified. The conclusions of this process are:

---

[1] Data obtained from https://www.policia.gov.co/grupo-informacion-criminalidad/estadistica-delictiva.

[2] Data obtained from https://datosabiertos.bogota.gov.co/dataset/sector-catastral.

[3] Data obtained from https://datosabiertos.bogota.gov.co/dataset/indice-de-condiciones-noc turnal.

- The most influential factors for the analysis of the crime of theft are place and time.
- In complement to the event place, it is important to include variables related to the surrounding sociocultural environment, number of security cameras, number of access roads, number of banks, and nearby stores.
- In complement to the event time, it is recommended to include variables for the season of the year, and also special dates and payment calendars.
- Concerning the victim, it would be important to include variables such as age, genre, physical conditions or if there is a disability.
- Related to the types of theft crimes, in order to obtain more significant rules, it is better to group them into two main categories: theft from people and theft from property.

The following section details the implementation of these recommendations made by the experts.

3.2 Consolidated Dataset

Due to some of the neighborhoods reported in the crimes being not legalized neighborhoods and some overlap, the Places API of Google maps was used to identify which *SCA* (*Cadastral Sector*) belongs to the neighborhoods where the theft crimes occurred and integrate the data sources 1 and 2 mentioned in the previous section. The SCA covers the entire surface of the area of Suba (see Fig. 1).

Then, applying the concepts of geometry and polygons, the centroid of the polygon of each *SCA* was calculated, and the median between the distances from the centroid to each of the points that make up the polygon was calculated. This median of the distance was used as a radius to perform the search through the Places API and thus find the bars, banks and ATMs, commercial stores, and parks, to build new variables for each *SCA*. *UPZs* are larger polygons that contain several *SCA*. Through these larger polygons, the *UPZ* area was calculated and compared to the *SCA* areas, to obtain the proportion of the safety indices of the *UPZ* for each individual *SCA*. From the date's variable, new variables were created as intervals or days of the week, such as business days or weekend. From the neighborhoods, new variables of characteristics were created as mentioned above. Due to the sensitivity and privacy of the personal data, it was not considered to include more specific information related to the victim variable. Table 1 shows the set of variables that were finally integrated into the consolidated dataset.

This concludes the consolidation of data as a differential factor of this project. This consolidated basis is used to build the association rules and then generate the recommendations.

Fig. 1. Polygons of the cadastral sectors that contain the different neighborhoods of the area of Suba in Bogotá.

Table 1. Description of the transformed variables and the new variables that make up the consolidated database.

Variable	Description	Factor
HOUR_INT	Time interval	Time
DAY_WEEK INT	Interval day of the week	Time
DAY_MONTH_INT	Day of the month interval	Time
MONTH	Month	Time
ACTIVITY	Activity at the crime scene	Place
SCA_AREA	SCA area	Place
DENSITY_BARS	Bar-based density	Place
DENSITY_BANKS	Bank-based density	Place
DENSITY_STORES	Trading-based density	Place
DENSITY_PARKS	Park-based density	Place
LIGHTING	Lighting index	Place

(*continued*)

Table 1. (*continued*)

Variable	Description	Factor
PEOPLE	Index of people	Place
SAFETY	Police index	Place
ROAD	Public trail index	Place
TRANSPORT	Transport index	Place
GENDER	Gender of the victim	Victim
CRIMES	Type of theft	Objective

4 Fuzzy Association Rules

With the consolidated database described in the previous section, the association rules are constructed using fuzzy linguistic variables. The use of fuzzy representation is used to address the problem found in the state of the art of the need to have a citizen-oriented approach and handle an understandable and interpretable language. This section starts with a theoretical introduction of the techniques applied, followed by an explanation of why and how they were applied in this project. The next section will explain how these rules can be used to generate recommendations by evaluating variations in the rules to identify those that minimize the risk of a citizen being a victim of theft.

4.1 Fuzzy Partitioning

The *Fuzzy Partitioning (FP)* operation consists of transforming the attributes of a given problem into attributes with fuzzy values, that is, defining for each attribute several fuzzy sets in the universe of discourse. So, if the attribute is continuous, the *fuzzification* process includes the discretization of that attribute.

In *fuzzy partitions*, the data value can belong to more than one partition with some membership level. This membership level can be derived using different membership functions. The fuzzy sets, in most real-life datasets, are triangular, trapezoidal, or Gaussian (see Fig. 2 as an example), according to the nature of each variable of the datasets.

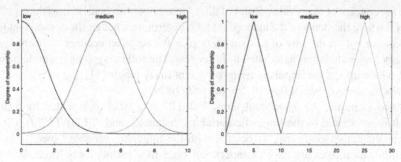

Fig. 2. Membership functions a) Gaussian b) Triangular [10].

The numeric data present in most real-life datasets can be converted to fuzzy sets using any of these membership functions, in which a particular data point can belong to two or more *fuzzy sets* simultaneously [10].

The *fuzzification* component or module of the recommendation model is responsible for receiving the pre-processed information. It consists of functions to normalize the data, group it by k-means, and calculate the membership function of the fuzzy set. The number of obtained groupings corresponds to the number of fuzzy sets (see Table 2). The clustering algorithm selects random points as the first 4 groups. Repeatedly allocates new clusters by averaging the assigned points until the points do not change to a new cluster. After grouping, each point now has its associated groups. The output is fuzzy data, which is the conversion of points to fuzzy sets using the triangular and trapezoidal functions, parametrized based on the obtained clusters.

Table 2. Linguistic variables represented by fuzzy sets for each of the variables.

Variable	Linguistic labels of the fuzzy sets
SCA_AREA	{Very Small, Small. Medium, Large}
DENSITY_BARS	{Very Low, Low. Medium, High}
DENSITY_BANKS	{Very Low, low. Medium, high}
DENSITY_STORES	{Very Low, low. Medium, high}
DENSITY_PARKS	{Very Low, low. Medium, high}
LIGHTING	{Very Low, low. Medium, high}
PEOPLE	{Very Low, low. Medium, high}
SAFETY	{Very Low, low. Medium, high}
ROAD	{Very Low, low. Medium, high}
TRANSPORT	{Very Low, Low. Medium, High}

4.2 Association Rules

To constitute a system based on rules that use properties of fuzzy sets, it is necessary to define the concept of fuzzy rules. Rules of this type are based on heuristics of the type "IF-THEN", where the items of the antecedent term determine whether the consequent term will occur or not. In the case of being a fuzzy rule, the terms antecedent and consequent are fuzzy linguistic labels associated to fuzzy sets. The following is an example of such a rule, where uppercase linguistic terms represent fuzzy labels [11].

if the distance is NEAR then the speed is SLOW

In this example, the antecedent term, "NEAR" is a label represented by a fuzzy set that is associated to the linguistic variable "distance", and "SLOWLY" is a fuzzy label, in the consequent term, associated with the linguistic variable "speed". In this way, implication rules are easy to understand since they include only linguistic terms very close to human language.

There are different algorithms for the creation of association rules. This model uses *FP-Growth* in which the process of inducing association rules works with a significantly smaller data structure than the traditional *Apriori* algorithm. The search for sets of frequent items is done only in an *FP-Tree* and not in the whole data set. In addition, the operation of *FP-Growth* is based on a strategy of divide and conquer. Thus, the search space traversed by the algorithm is significantly smaller. Experiments showed that *FP-Growth* is faster and more scalable than the *Apriori* algorithm [12]. This advantages are related to the fact that as the support threshold decreases, the frequency of items increases. The sets of candidates that the *Apriori* algorithm must handle become extremely large, and matching patterns with many candidates by searching transactions becomes very expensive.

The association rules conform to the objectives of this project since they allow us to find relationships and patterns of occurrence, easily generate variations in the rules, and look for alternative rules that can minimize the risk of the crime of theft. The quality measures used to find the best rules are as follows:

- *Support:* frequency of occurrence of the rule.
- *Confidence:* the likelihood that the result will appear given the background.
- *Number of wildcards:* number of variables that can be changed in the rule antecedent, for example, the day and time.
- *Number of antecedents:* the rule's number of antecedents.
- *Membership:* AND operation of rule memberships for fuzzy value.

5   Recommendation Model

Once the fuzzy association rules have been obtained, as shown in the previous section, the recommendations are generated by making variations on the users' queries and looking for similar rules that minimize the theft risk. The following sections explain how to produce and interpret the recommendations, followed by the complete step-by-step process that is used to generate the recommendations.

5.1   Interpretation of Recommendations

To generate the recommendations and take into account the requirement of having a focus on citizens, the fuzzy association rules presented in the previous section are used; in fact, having linguistic labels can be intuitive and easy to understand. The rules that best match a user's input query are identified and the risk level is calculated. The user's query includes temporal and spatial information. A query can be interpreted as a scenario related to an activity that would be done by a user. The idea is to find similar alternative scenarios with lower risk level that could be recommended to the user.

Once the rules that are similar to the user's query have been identified, different small variations of the conditions of the query are tested to find alternative options with a lower risk level. To create the variations, the concept of *wildcard* variables has been used. Variables such as neighborhood, date and time, and site of the activity can be modified to try to find a better security situation. The variations are made on the rules by changing the components of the rule antecedent and verifying if there is a rule to evaluate its quality measures to find those that minimize the theft risk. Although the gender variable is included as an input value and used to find the rules, it is not considered a *wildcard* because it is not possible to recommend users to modify their gender.

The recommendation process is illustrated in the following example. A user enters a query that she is a woman who will visit the Pasadena neighborhood today at 20 h and will be making some purchases in a shopping area. As a recommendation, the system suggest that she change the time of day for an hour in the morning, so her risk level would go from being high to low. Another possible recommendation would be to change the neighborhood because its bank density is very high; in a neighborhood that has a lower bank density, the risk of being a victim of theft is lower. Depending on her context, the user can decide which recommendation could be applied.

5.2 Recommendation Process

The flow to making a recommendation begins with the entry provided by the user, which is a query including the data related to gender, neighborhood, date and time, and place where the activity will be carried out. These variables were chosen because, using them, the other derived variables are constructed, as was explained in Sect. 3. In addition, when searching for the rules, more candidate rules are found. On the other hand, with these variables, you can identify what activity a user will perform outside the home and answer the questions of whom, how, when, and where. After this, the RMFAR model makes the recommendations and returns to the user the 10 recommendations that most minimize the risk of being a victim of theft. The recommendations give information suggesting modifying the value of a user's query data item to reduce the thief risk; for example, see Fig. 3, if the schedule is changed, the risk becomes low with feasibility or a score of 0.34.

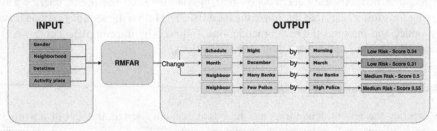

Fig. 3. Input and output process for RMFAR.

The process for generating recommendations (see Fig. 4) begins with the user data input and the generation, preprocessing, and creation of new variables from the Places API as described in Sect. 3. Then a fuzzy partitioning is performed to assign linguistic labels to each piece of data, followed by changing the values of the *wildcards* in the input data, searching for the new rules, and calculating the difference between the risk scores. Finally, the recommendations that minimize the risk of the crime of theft are returned.

Equation 1 is used to identify the candidate rules to be considered in this process. This weighting calculation uses the rule quality measures introduced in the preceding

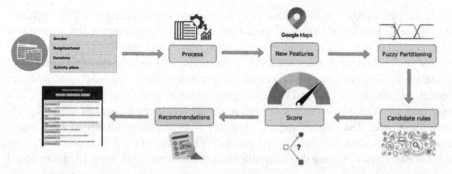

Fig. 4. Process flow from data input to the generation of recommendations.

section. The weighting coefficients used in the experimental test of the system are shown in Table 3. The best performance was achieved using the weighting coefficients equal to 0.25 for all criteria.

$$rule.weigth = w_1 \; x \; rule.support + w_2 \; x \; rule.confidence + w_3 \; x \; rule.antecedents \\ + w_4 \; x \; rule.wildcards$$

$$(1)$$

Table 3. Fuzzy sets for each of the variables with discrete values.

Weight ID	Criteria	Value
w_1	Rule support	0.25
w_2	Rule trust	0.25
$w3$	Background size	0.25
w_4	Number of wildcards	0.25

The membership level of a fuzzy rule, in which the antecedent is expressed as a conjunction, is calculated using the min operator applied to the membership levels of the input linguistic variables. The rule risk score is then calculated using the rule weight and the rule fuzzy membership level (Eq. 2).

$$rule.score = rule.weigth \; x \; 0.5 + rule.membership \; x \; 0.5 \qquad (2)$$

6 Evaluation

The evaluation of the model is supported by 2 types of validations. The first focused on evaluating the quality of the rules by comparing them against another analytical model. The second focused on measuring the acceptance of the system by users and experts.

In the first validation, in addition to evaluating the model based on FP-Growth, the evaluation of a different analytical model was carried out, to compare the behavior of the proposed model. The alternative model used was a Decision Tree *(DT)*, which also allows you to find rules from a CRISP perspective. The evaluation of the analytical models is carried out through a controlled experiment. The independent variables are gender, neighborhood, date and time, and place of the activity. The dependent variables measured are rule weight, rule score, score difference, precision, recall, accuracy, f1-score, and time. The intervening variables are hyperparameters such as max depth, min sample, percentage of training, percentage of tests, and weighting coefficients. This experimental protocol using these variables was implemented by testing 12 experimental scenarios.

The results obtained can be seen in Table 4. The accuracy of the models is greater than 50%. The best accuracy (0.5735) for the Decision Tree model was obtained by adjusting hyperparameters with 70% of the data for training and 30% for testing. On the other hand, the best accuracy (0.55) for the RMFAR model was obtained with the weighting coefficients of the same value as 0.25 for the criteria defined above and with 70% of the data for training and 30% for tests. The difference in performance between the two models is minimal, but the RMFAR has the advantage of generating fuzzy rules that are more appropriate for the type of application.

As for the execution time, a big difference can be observed between the 2 models in general. The longest time of the decision tree model was 4.81 ms and the lowest was 3.1 ms. This is because the recommendation model generates many rules, which makes its processing quite heavy. Considering that the purpose of the model is to generate recommendations based on the fuzzy association rules, a model that contemplates many rules allows us to generate more accurate recommendations and a larger variety of recommendations.

Table 4. Results of the best experiments comparing the RMFAR, and the Decision Tree models.

Model	Train	Test	Precision	Recall	F1-Score	Time	Accuracy
RMFAR1	70%	30%	0.53	0.56	0.55	4 min 39 s	0.55
RFMAR5	80%	20%	0.53	0.56	0.55	4 min 36 s	0.55
DTREE3	70%	30%	0.59	0.45	0.51	3.1 ms	0.5713
DTREE4	80%	20%	0.62	0.38	0.46	3.15 ms	0.5735

For the evaluation of the model's acceptance, the *Technological Acceptance Model (TAM)* was used. A prototype and an evaluation questionnaire were presented to experts and users to evaluate the *Perceived Utility (PU),* Perceived Ease of *Use (PEU)*, and Attitude towards *Use (AU)* w. A more detailed description of these acceptance criteria is presented in Table 5.

We used the Likert scale where 1 disagrees and 5 is totally in agreement, and the questionnaires were applied to 15 citizens and 4 experts. The obtained results are summarized in Fig. 5. From the results of this test, it is demonstrated that the proposed model

Table 5. Indicators used for TAM evaluation.

Indicator	Description
PU	The degree to which a person believes that using the system will highlight him or his performance at work
PEU	The degree to which a person believes that by using the system they will free themselves from stress
AU	Indicates the link between the effort expended to use and the benefits of the use of the system

meets the minimum required quality criteria. The evaluators consider that in addition to being useful, the *RMFAR* model would increase knowledge about the actions citizens should take to mitigate the risk of being victims of theft crime.

On the other hand, they find great ease of use since it is a simple system and that it would not take long to adapt to the process. The only aspect that is found to have a neutral response is the response time of the system; in fact, the large amount of data that the model considers affects the immediate response time.

After the evaluations and recommendations of the evaluators, it was concluded, that the model is useful enough and capable of generating recommendations that can help citizens mitigate the risks of being victims of theft crime.

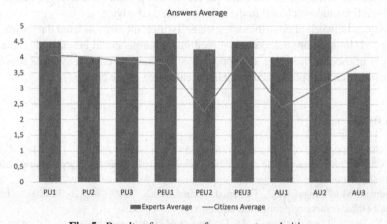

Fig. 5. Results of responses from experts and citizens.

7 Conclusions and Future Work

The use of open information sources makes it possible to deduce data such as densities of nightlife, banking, and commercial establishments. Having a greater amount of information allows you to use fuzzy logic and obtain much more precise rules. This work makes a novel contribution because the work carried out considered various sources of information. However, it should be noted that the construction of this unified database is subject to the availability of updated data published by the government entities in charge of citizen security issues.

Through *fuzzy logic,* fuzzy association rules were constructed that allowed one to break the limitations of the use of *CRISP data,* proposed in most of the previous works, and to use a language more adapted to the real world, thus having a closer approach to the citizens.

The *accuracy* compared to other models was acceptable for the context of the project but could be improved if more complete information about the citizen is available, as recommended by the experts. Although this accuracy is not so high, the recommendations obtained are good enough because they are calculated through variations on a query made by the user. This way to generate the recommendation by looking for variations of rules is a novel contribution, since a recommendation model with such an approach had not been used in the previous works. The results of the TAM show good acceptance of the proposed solution. However, some aspects can be improved.

Future work shall include data related to the victim, although care must be taken because most of this data is sensitive and difficult to access. Changing multiple wild-cards in the rules could lead to better rules that help generate more accurate and useful recommendations. Suggesting more specific ways to achieve a recommendation, such as indicating, for instance, the nearest neighborhood given the characteristics of the user's query, was not within the scope of the project. Including this type of additional context-based information would make the recommendations more useful thanks to the additional information included in the solution-oriented advice.

Through a network of contributors, such as Twitter, the consolidated database could be expanded. In addition, the system of recommendations could be expanded to cover other areas of the city; however, the approach of specialized-context systems should be maintained by having specialized models for each area of the city.

References

1. DANE. Encuesta de Convivencia y Seguridad Ciudadana del DANE (2019). Colombia (2019). https://www.dane.gov.co/index.php/estadisticas-por-tema/seguridad-y-defensa/encuesta-de-convivencia-y-seguridad-ciudadana-ecsc. Accessed 07 May 2021
2. Friedman, M., Grawert, A.C., Cullen, J.: Crime trends: 1990–2016, 1–36 (2017). https://www.brennancenter.org/publication/crime-trends1990-2016
3. Hu, X., Wu, J., Chen, P., Sun, T., Li, D.: Impact of climate variability and change on crime rates in Tangshan, China. Sci. Total Environ. **609**, 1041-1048 (2017). https://doi.org/10.1016/j.scitotenv.2017.07.163
4. Shah, N., Bhagat, N., Shah, M.: Crime forecasting: a machine learning and computer vision approach to crime prediction and prevention. Vis. Comput. Ind. Biomed. Art **4**(1), 1–14 (2021). https://doi.org/10.1186/s42492-021-00075-z
5. Giménez-Santana, A., Caplan, J.M., Drawve, G.: Risk terrain modeling and socio-economic stratification: identifying risky places for violent crime victimization in Bogotá, Colombia. Eur. J. Crim. Policy Res. **24**(4), 417–431 (2018). https://doi.org/10.1007/s10610-018-9374-5

6. Ordóñez, H., Cobos, C., Bucheli, V.: Machine learning model for predicting theft trends in Colombia|Machine learning model for the prediction of theft trends in Colombia, RISTI - Rev. Iber. Sist. and Tecnol. Inf. **2020**(E29), 494–506 (2020)

7. Gélvez-ferreira, J.D., Paula, M., Rodríguez, N.: Archivos de economía (2021)

8. Zhang, Y., Siriaraya, P., Kawai, Y., Jatowt, A.: Time and location recommendation for crime prevention. In: Bakaev, M., Frasincar, F., Ko, I.-Y. (eds.) ICWE 2019. LNCS, vol. 11496, pp. 47–62. Springer, Cham (2019). https://doi.org/10.1007/978-3-030-19274-7_4

9. Englin, R.: Indirect association rule mining for crime data analysis (2015)

10. Ramdasi, S.: Interpretability of fuzzy clusters by fuzzy association rules using cluster based fuzzy partitioning. **5**(4), 333–347 (2016)

11. Lucas, J.P.: Association-based classification methods applied to recommendation systems, Thesis Dr. Univ. Salamanca (2010). https://www.mendeley.com/catalog/métodos-clasificació n-basados-en-asociacion-aplicados-sistemas-recomendación/?utm_source=desktop&utm_ medium=1.14&utm_campaign=open_catalog&userDocumentId=%7B0266e5d0-3c99-48c8-aa76-fda6ff9bbd18%7D

12. Han, J., Pei, J., Yin, Y.: Mining frequent patterns without candidate generation. ACM SIGMOD Rec. **29**(2) (2000). https://doi.org/10.1145/335191.335372

Implementing a Deep Learning Algorithm for Detection of Denial of Service Attacks

Juan Fernando Cañola Garcia[1] (ID) and Gabriel Enrique Taborda Blandon[2(✉)] (ID)

[1] Grupo Éxito S.A, 055428 Envigado, Colombia
juancanola116639@correo.itm.edu.co
[2] Instituto Tecnológico Metropolitano, 050036 Medellín, Colombia
gabrieltaborda@itm.edu.co

Abstract. This article presents the advances obtained in a research on the application of artificial intelligence (AI) techniques for the detection of denial of service (DoS). The investigation begins with the analysis of Machine Learning and Deep Learning techniques used to recognize DoS attacks, and then continues with the selection, training and classification of an algorithm for DoS detection. From the work carried out, it was possible to identify the artificial neural network Deep Feed Forward, which is a Deep Learning (DL) algorithm, which shows a very promising behavior to detect DoS attacks. For model training, the CICDDoS2019 data set was adapted, this data set contains twelve types of packages; eleven are DoS attacks and the twelfth belongs to benign or normal packets. The precision obtained was 0.7293, for the DL in-put model that recognizes 11 types of DoS attacks.

Keywords: Denial of service attack · Deep learning · Intruder detection system · Neural networks

1 Introduction

In computers system security the problems have increased exponentially in recent decades, as seen in the reports of cybersecurity companies. With the conditions by the COVID-19 pandemic, where organizations had to implement their business activities and tasks virtually, computer security issues have become severe and a daily concern for businesses and individuals about how to protect their information technologies (IT) assets. As a way of illustration, some statistics will be cited, which show the current critical situation of this problem:

Cybercrime has grown by 600% since the beginning of the pandemic and it is predicted that the global costs for this type of crime will amount to 6 trillion dollars, making it one of the most profitable illegal activities worldwide. In addition, cybersecurity spending will exceed $60 million in 2021 and according to Cybint Solutions, only 38% of companies globally mention that they are prepared for a largescale attack. On the other hand, cybercriminals no longer distinguish between large and small companies, the company Verizon states in its report shows 43% of data breaches in 2019 involved attacks

E. Gonzalez et al. (Eds.): CCC 2021, CCIS 1594, pp. 46–64, 2022.
https://doi.org/10.1007/978-3-031-19951-6_4

on small businesses. In addition, according to the National Cybersecurity Alliance, 88% of small business owners believe hackers would attack them and a quarter of small and medium sized businesses would see business continuity compromised by such an event [2].

One of the attacks that has had a significant growth in times of pandemic, is the denial of services, according to a research conducted by GlobeNet, in 2020 its customers have suffered an increase of 300% of DoS attack, compared with 2019 [10]. DoS attacks are intended to disable or slow down the provision of a computer system, application or computer machine, making a large number of requests or connections simultaneously. As can be concluded, this type of attacks is highly harmful to any organization or company, since its objective is to block the provision of the service.

The computer security technique to mitigate DoS attacks is known as intrusion detection consists of identifying the presence of unauthorized users trying to access a computer network. To detect intruders, different tools and techniques are used to analyze traffic on the network and thus detect strange behaviors, with the aim of protecting information and avoiding consequences [3]. There are basically two strategies for intrusion detection. One is known signature-based; consists of detecting intruders from a database of signatures or indicators created from previous attacks. In addition, the other strategy is known as anomaly-detection; which detects the intruder from the monitoring, collection and analysis of the packets of the network, for a subsequent analysis and classification into a normal behavior or an anomalous behavior [22].

Although the efforts made by companies and computer security experts, the computer systems remain objective of cyber-attacks, these breaches continue to grow exponentially. In addition, given the capacity of evolution, change and adaptation that cybercriminals have to plan to launch their attacks, practically make them unpredictable to DoS attacks, given the uncertainty of time, place, form and technique used in their execution, allowing them to be characterized as complex. The purpose of this study is, thus, to propose an intrusion detection method that helps mitigate DoS attacks. We opted for an intrusion detection system based on anomalies, using an technique of Artificial Intelligence (AI), such as neural networks, which are able to learn, thanks to a massive set of data (Dataset) that allows to train an algorithm, in this case designed for the detection of DoS attacks, allowing a computer system to remain alert about possible threats. Subsequently, thanks to the new data it processes, this machine is training increasingly to improve its classification and identify new attacks [22].

The rest of this paper is structured as follows: Sect. 2 presents the conceptual framework; where the most relevant concepts related to the topic are exposed. Sections 3 provides the background of Machine Learning and Deep Learning regarding intrusion detection; this section presents in succinct form the works reported in the scientific literature related to this research. Section 4 presents the methodology used to achieve the proposed objective. Section 5 the results obtained by applying the proposed methodologist. Section 6 draws with the conclusion and future work.

2   Conceptual Framework

In this section, the most relevant conceptual supports of this research are detailed, starting with DoS attacks and then with the neural network techniques used in this project.

2.1 Denial of Service

Denial of Service (DoS) and Distributed Denial of Service (DDoS) are computer security attacks that primarily target computing resources (CPU, RAM, or bandwidth) of a device or network to disable access to legitimate users. These attacks can be classified into two types:

- *Exploits*: which consists of exploiting software flaws to affect performance.
- *Flooding*: where the attacker sends a large number of fake network packets to affect bandwidth or device resources. The types of attack in which it is divided are: single source and multiple source, the latter is subdivided into Zombies and Reflectors.

Distributed-denial-of-service (DDoS) is a special type of DoS, in which various devices connected in the network are used to increase the threat level, distributing denial-of-service attacks from different sources, either exploiting software flaws or sending a number of fake packets. The methods used to perform a distributed denial of service. DDoS attacks are classified into two types:

- Decrease in bandwidth. This type of attack consists of flooding and saturating the victim's network with malicious or unwanted traffic preventing legitimate traffic from reaching its destination. This type of attack is subdivided into two: flooding, where the network is saturated by sending malicious packets from different devices and the other type is amplification, in which broadcast messages are sent from different sources with the spoofed IP, where the spoofed IP is the victim's IP.
- Resource decrease. This type of attack consists of saturating the resources of the victim's system, making the system unable to process legitimate requests. This type of attack is subdivided into two: exploit protocols, where vulnerabilities of communication protocols are exploited and malformed packet attacks, where the attacker sends a massive amount of non-legitimate packets from different sources [12].

2.2 Detection Techniques Against DoS Attacks

Figure 1 details the different methods of each of the techniques. Detection against DoS attacks can be classified into three techniques:

- *Anomalies*, used to detect unknown DoS attacks from the monitoring, collection and analysis of network packets.
- *Signatures*, used for DoS attacks through signatures or indicators of known attacks.
- *Hybrids* that uses both techniques.

2.3 Artificial Intelligence Learning Techniques

Machine Learning. Broadly speaking is a way to teach an electronic device how to detect patterns from a large amount of data. Machine Learning is used in different fields of computing such as: computer vision, medicine, video games, social media marketing, where its superiority has been demonstrated, compared to traditional programs based on a set of defined rules. In addition, in recent years, Machine Learning is also being integrated into cyber detection systems to support or even replace computer security experts [6].

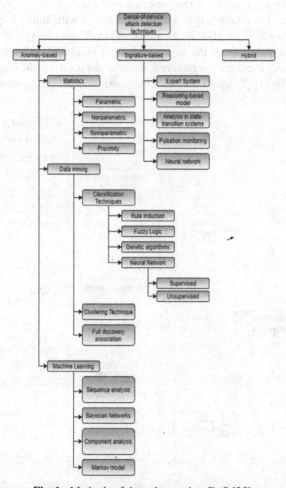

Fig. 1. Methods of detection against DoS [25].

Deep Learning. Deep Learning is an enhanced machine learning technique, which performs its operations using multiple layers and neurons. These layers are interconnected and each layer composed of neurons receives the output of the neurons of the previous layer as input. Deep Learning has been used in areas such as: image processing, natural language processing, customer relationship automation, autonomous vehicle systems, among others, showing itself as one of the relevant technologies of this era.

2.4   Classification of Machine Learning Algorithms for Cybersecurity

The Machine Learning algorithms used in the area of computer security is classified into two types: Shallow Learning and Deep Learning.

Shallow Learning, requires a feature extraction expert to map data from network inputs. In contrast, Deep Learning is a multilayer model with ability to perform feature extraction on its own. Both algorithms are subdivided into two types: supervised and unsupervised, the difference is the supervised, their outputs (labels) are known, while in the unsupervised; these are not required, because the users are the ones who interpret the results [6]. The Fig. 2 details the Machine Learning methods used in cybersecurity.

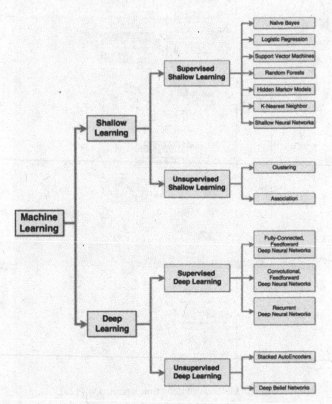

Fig. 2. Machine Learning Methods for cibersecurity [6]

2.5   Dataset

A Dataset is a set of related data exploited by an organization's information systems and have been used in recent years to train models of Machine Learning and Deep Learning. Currently, the most challenging to optimize the performance of detection systems against DoS is to find the right data, because according to this, the model performs a better classification. One way to get a Dataset, is by analyzing and collecting the information from the network, but this is expensive. The other way is to use public Datasets available on the internet. The Dataset used in this research is the DDoS Evaluation Dataset CICDDoS2019 [18], developed by the Canadian Institute for Cybersecurity. This Dataset is containing 11 types of DoS attacks and 1 benign or non-malicious traffic. Table 3 shows the types of attacks from Dataset. In addition, it contains 88 features for each record as source IP, destination IP, source port, destination port, protocol, etc. In addition, researchers from the Canadian Institute for Cyber-security, who created this Dataset, conducted research to learn about the most relevant features of each DoS attack, resulting in 22 features.

3 Previous Jobs

This section briefly describes some of the papers published in the scientific literature and that are related to this research.

Researchers from the Center for Information Security of the University of Beijing conducted a study where they summarize the methods of Machine Learning and Deep Learning for the detection of intrusions in the network [22]. In this paper, after having made the comparison of the different methods, they concluded that there is no more effective method for detection, because each one of the methods to detect anomalies has advantages and disadvantages. In addition, they add that the Methods of Machine Learning and Deep Learning do not work properly without the corresponding Dataset, and to date of the publication, the available Datasets present several drawbacks either by outdated or unequal in the number of records, and creating a new one represents a great consumption of time.

On the other hand, Nvaporn and Vasaka [9], presented in their research, an intrusion detection technique using a Deep Learning model which can classify different types of attacks without being explicitly programmed. To verify the performance, they used a Dataset called MAWI which are pcap files and compares the result with IDS snort. In the study, they mention that they experimented with a model with 1000 epochs, at a learning rate between 0.01 and 0.5. Its variants showed significant performance com-pared to Machine Learning classifiers. The three Deep Learning methods that they obtained detect different types of attacks with a score of 1 without accessing the payload, only with information from the header, being the Recurrent Neural Network (RNN) algorithm the one with the best results in terms of Accuracy. To validate the detection operation, they implemented the models in a controlled environment. The researchers say the next step is to implement it in a real-time environment.

In the research Priyadarshini y Barik [7], describe how they trained a model using the Long Short Term Memory (LSTM) algorithm. The Hogzilla Dataset and the ISCX 2012 Dataset were used for the training. The LSTM network has been configured with 3 hidden layers, 1 dense layer, 128 input nodes and a dropout of 0.2 for all hidden layers, giving a good performance indicator in terms of increasing accuracy and reduced error rate. The final model achieved a performance in the Accuracy of 98.88%. In demonstrating how the models work, the researchers modified the packet flow using a software-defined network, equipping the DDoS attack defense module with the trained model, in this way, infected packets are denied by the network, preventing denial of service from spreading.

In the work of Bhuvaneswari y Selvakumar [17], demonstrated a strategy for detecting denial-of-service attacks they called DeeRal (Deep Radial Intelligence) with a weight optimizer known as CUI (Cumulative Incarnation), using neural networks, the RBF (Radial basis function) activation function, and the KDD and UNSW NB15 NSL Datasets for model training. The model trained with the neural network and CUI optimizer obtained the best Accuracy of 99.69. The article compares the result with other DoS attack detection strategies, but does not demonstrate its application in specific cases; it does not show future work to be done with this strategy.

In the research conducted by Zouhair, Noredinne, Khalid, Amina, Mohamed [8], developed a Network Intruder Detection System (NIDS) using Deep Learning based on genetic algorithms and simulated cooling algorithm. They obtained a performance in the Accuracy of 99.92%. As future work, they propose to adapt the proposed strategy to detect intruders by analyzing encrypted packets.

In another study [13], implemented an IDS based on a recurrent neural network algorithm called Deep Long short term Memory. The performance in the Accuracy obtained was 99.51%. The article compares the results with other Machine Learning methods, showing a significant increase in performance. As future work, they plan to study the performance of each attack found in the NSL-KDD Dataset.

On the other hand [19], developed a training of different machine learning algorithms supervised using own datasets and others obtained from the internet to detect Low Type DoS attacks. The algorithms they implemented to train the model were Logistic Regression, KNN, SVM, Decision Trees, Random Forest, and Deep Neural Network. The performance in the Accuracy obtained was 98.75%. According to the researchers, the main objective of the work was to demonstrate whether the parameters of TCP packets could be used as features to detect Low Denial of Service (LDoS) attacks. The main limitation of the research was the Datasets used, because some are simulated data, and therefore, as future work it is intended to use real data. Another limitation was the hardware resources that prevented increasing the number of layers to achieve better performance, and also the lack of more data that could allow the creation of more models applicable to more server configurations and contents.

Narayanavadivoo and Selvakumar [5] implemented a technique for DoS detection called VCDeepFL (Vector Convolutional Deep Feature Learning). This technique is developed with the combination of two Deep Learning algorithms: Vector Convolutional Neural Network (VCNN) and Fully Connected Neural Network (FCNN). The performance obtained in the Accuracy was 99.3%. The study does not demonstrate the implementation of the detection system in a test environment, so it only remains in the testing phase of training. As future work, the researchers propose extracting rules from the VCDeepFL network for each class in the Dataset and making interpretation easier.

In the study conducted by Khuphiran, Leelaprute, Uthayopas and all [14], they developed a model with the Deep Learning algorithm called Deep Feed forward using the Darpa Intrusion Detection dataset. They managed to detect DoS attacks with an Accuracy of 99.63. According to the article, the operation of the models in a test environment is not demonstrated, so the researchers propose as future work to use the algorithm in a real-time data network.

In another research [23], they implemented an intrusion detection system using Deep Learning. The neural network is composed of Gated Recurrent unit (GRU), Perceptron multilayer (MLP) and the softmax module. For the training phase, they used the KDD and KDD 99 NSL Datasets, with which they obtained a 99.42% Accuracy performance to detect DOS attacks. According to the article, the proposed system only stays in theory and requires engineering work to put it into practice, so they propose that the next step would be to optimize the system so that it can be applied in real world environments.

Researchers Kasun, Kevin y Milos [4] developed a framework for anomaly detection using the NSL-KDD Dataset and the Deep Feed forward algorithm. The Accuracy obtained was 98.6217%. The researchers mention the detection system is in the process of being implemented and propose as future work, to provide information about the predictions made by the framework.

In another study [1], they used the NSL-KDD Dataset for Deep Learning-based DoS detection. Two experiments were conducted in the study. First, the neural network detected DDoS attacks with a classification accuracy of 0.988 using all features of the Dataset. In the second, the number of features was reduced to 24, which classified DoS attacks with an Accuracy of 0.984. In their future work, they propose to increase the number of DoS attacks to put the model into operation in different environments and of course in a real productive environment.

Researchers [21] used the methods of Machine Learning Random Forest and Deep Learning LSTM, to identify DoS attacks. The result showed that the Deep Learning algorithm performs better than a Machine Learning algorithm. The accuracy performance obtained with the LSTM algorithm was 97.606%. As future work, they propose to increase the diversity of DDoS attacks and system configurations to test the model in different environments and in a real-world environment. They also propose to build a system based on the model created and propose the creation of a new Dataset to publicize the new challenges in the identification of DDoS attacks.

In research conducted by Tae-Young Kim and Sung-Bae Cho [15], they implemented a Deep Learning algorithm for anomaly detection combining convolutional neural network and LSTM methods. The model achieved a performance in the Accuracy of 98.6%. The method has a delay in detecting anomalies with real data, due to the preprocessing that is required with the new data and which represents a challenge for future work.

According to the systematic review of the literature of Deep Learning algorithms for the detection of denial of service attacks, Table 1 was obtained; where it is condensed in a matrix the Accuracy and the references of scientific publications on Deep Learning algorithms and the Datasets used for training the classification models.

Table 1. Accuracy matrix of algorithms Vs dataset, according to the literature review.

Dataset / Algorithms	MawiLab 2017	ISCX 2012	NSLKDD	UNSW NB15	CICIDS2017	CNTC 2017	CSIC 2010	DARPA 1998	Netflow	KDD CUP 99	Darpa 2009 DDoS	Yahoo S5 Web	Dataset propio SSE
Recurrent Neural Network	100 [9]		98.8 [22]							99.49 [20]			
Convolutional Neural Network	100 [9]					94,11 [16]		99,36 [16]	99.41 [22]				
Stacked Recurrent Neural Network	100 [9]												
Long short Term Memory		98,88 [7]	99,51 [13]			95,12 [16]	96,13 [16]	99,98 [16]		99.8 [22]			
Deep Radial Intelligence			99,69 [17]	96,15 [17]									
Genetic Algorithm(Simulated Annealing Algorithm (SAA)					99.92 [8]								
VCNN/FNN			99.2 [5]										
Deep Belief Network			97.5 [22]						97.6 [22]	93.49 [22]			
Gradient Recurrent Unit									84.15 [22]				
Deep Feed Forward			93.78 [4]								99.63 [14]		
(Bidirectional Gradient Recurrent Unit)BGRU + MLP			99.24 [23]							99.84 [23]			
Restricted Boltzmann Machine			73.23 [11]							92,12 [24]			
CNN + LSTM												98.6 [15]	
AutoEncoders										91,86 [24]			98,99 [24]
Deep Defense(CNN, RNN, LSTM, GRU)		97,60 [24]											

4   Research Methodology

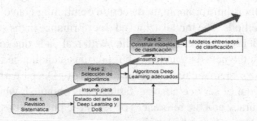

Fig. 3. Phases of research methodology

This section describes procedures, scientific techniques, and other strategies used during research. The Fig. 3 shows the phases of the methodology used.

4.1   Phase 1: Conducting a Systematic Literature Review (SLR)

With the intention of making a comparison between the different algorithms and Dataset used for detection DoS attacks published in the different investigations, a systematic literature review was developed in different recognized scientific databases on the methods of Deep Learning, Machine Learning and DoS attacks in a time window from 2009 to 2020. To carry out the review, the following steps were proposed:

- Specify research questions for systematic literature review.
- Define the search terms to filter on the databases.
- Choose scientific databases.
- Delimit the criteria for inclusion and exclusion of works.
- Perform the assessment of the quality of the research selected in the previous step.
- Analysis of the works that meet the quality criteria and contributes to this research.

4.2 Phase 2: Selection of Algorithms

This phase details the process for selecting the appropriate algorithms for identifying DoS attacks, using the following steps:

Selection of AI Learning Technique. Based on the analysis of the scientific literature review, it is necessary to define which of the techniques of artificial intelligence neural networks from Machine Learning or Deep Learning, is best suited to the detection of intruders and be able to prevent DoS.

Algorithm Selection Criteria. The matrix of Algorithms vs Datasets (Table 1) contains the list of Deep Learning algorithms for DoS detection found in the systematic literature review from the previous step. From these algorithms, the most suitable ones were selected, according to the definition of four criteria, which made possible the development of this research. The criteria defined are listed in Table 5, in the results section.

Implementation of Algorithms. With the appropriate algorithms selected, the training of the model proposed by researchers Aysegulsngr and Hacibeyoglu [1] was replicated using the Java Deep Learning 4J library and the NSLKDD Dataset. Of the three algorithms met the selection criteria, the latter was chosen, for the reasons stated in the results section and, in addition, because it was a reference configuration for the training of the various models that were implemented with the selected Dataset CICDDoS2019.

4.3 Phase 3: Building the Classification Models

The Fig. 4 describes the phase 3 process for building the classification models using Deep Learning. Below is each of the steps for building the classification models:

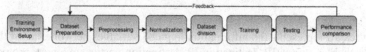

Fig. 4. Step sequence diagram for phase 3

Training Environment Setup. The training environment is composed for the Debian operating system, which is an operating system that consumes few resources, which are used for training. Table 2 describes the specifications of the server used for training.

Table 2. Training server features

Component	Specification
Processor	Intel Xeon 1.90 GHz 64 kl bit, 8 cores
RAM	32GB DDR4 2666
Hard drive	Magnetic 100 GB
Operating system	Debian 10
IDE	eclipse
Frameworks	Java 1.8, DL4J

Dataset Preparation. The Dataset selected to train the models was the DDoS Evaluation Dataset CICDDoS2019. This Dataset contains millions of records (48,099,733) of exclusively DoS attacks. As shown in Table 3, this dataset is divided into 11 files.

Table 3. Description of the CICDDoS2019 dataset

Files from Dataset			Dataset DDoS Attacks		
Name	**Size**	**Number of records**			
DrDoS_DNSFile	2.0 GiB	5074414	Testing Set	PortMap	09:43 - 09:51
				NetBIOS	10:00 - 10:09
DrDoS_LDAPFile	874.8 MiB	218153		LDAP	10:21 - 10:30
				MSSQL	10:33 - 10:42
DrDoS_MSSQLFile	1.8 GiB	4524499		UDP	10:53 - 11:03
				UDP-Lag	11:14 - 11:24
DrDoS_NetBIOSFile	1.6 GiB	4094987		SYN	11:28 - 17:35
DrDoS_NTPFile	615.1 MiB	1217008	Training Set	NTP	10:35 - 10:45
				DNS	10:52 - 11:05
DrDoS_SNMPFile	2.0 GiB	5161378		LDAP	11:22 - 11:32
				MSSQL	11:36 - 11:45
DrDoS_SSDPFile	1.2 GiB	2611375		NetBIOS	11:50 - 12:00
				SNMP	12:12 - 12:23
DrDoS_UDPFile	1.4 GiB	3136803		SSDP	12:27 - 12:37
				UDP	12:45 - 13:09
SynFile	607.8 MiB	1582682		UDP-Lag	13:11 - 13:15
				WebDDoS (ARME)	13:18 - 13:29
TFTPFile	8.7 GiB	20107828		SYN	13:29 - 13:34
UDPLagFile	150.7 MiB	370606		TFTP	13:35 - 17:15

Each record represents the information in an 88 variables network packet that contains data such as source IP, destination IP, destination port, source port, protocol, and so on. The last column in each record represents the type of DoS attack to which each record belongs. If a record is not part of a DoS attack, it is listed as BENIGN. According to the study conducted by the Canadian Institute for Cybersecurity, there are 22 relevant variables out of 88, with respect to how important each variable is for each type of DoS attack [18].

Dataset Preprocessing. The training algorithm requires labels variables (neural network output values) to be numerical. Therefore, since they are given in the form of a string in the dataset, outputs labels are associated with a number for each label of the attack and the benign traffic as shown in the Table 4.

Table 4. Labels of the output layer

Number	Label	Number	Label	Number	Label	Number	Label
0	BENIGN	4	MSSQL	8	UDP	12	WebDDoS
1	NTP	5	NETBIOS	9	UDP-LAG		
2	DNS	6	SNMP	10	SYN		
3	LDAP	7	SSDP	11	TFTP		

Dataset Normalization. Neural networks work best when the data are normalized, that is, it is restricted between a range between −1 and 1. The reasons for this is that neural networks are trained using the gradient descent and their activation functions usually have an active range between −1 and 1. For this research, all 22 features were restricted to this range to improve performance.

Dataset Division. The Dataset was randomly divided with java code into 2; one part used for training and the other part used in performance testing. The percentage of data allocated for training is 90% of the data and the other 10% for testing. It is clarified that in many references they recommend using a proportion of 70% for training and 30%, it was changed to obtain a better training of the model.

Training. Training. Various settings were used to find the best performance. This is achieved by modifying hyperparameters such as the amount of data, the batch size, the number of layers, the number of neurons, and the epochs. In total, 28 classification models were created, the results obtained are in Table 8.

Trained Model Testing. Once the training phase of the models was completed, the trained model was stored in a.bin file. For the testing phase, each model is loaded and evaluated with 10% of the records in the Dataset reserved for testing. The performance measures of the trained Deep Learning models taken as a reference are Accuracy, Precision, Recall and F1 Score.

Model performance comparison. After testing each trained model, the results were tabulated and a comparison was made, based on the measurements taken as a reference. This comparison allowed evaluating the performance of each model and making modifications to the hyper parameters in order to obtain the most efficient model. Table 8 shows the results in each of the models performed in this phase.

5 Results

5.1 Phase 1: Conducting a Systematic Literature Review (SLR)

The synthesis of the results obtained in the systematic literature review phase can be found in section two *Conceptual Framework* and section three *Previous Jobs* of this article. The steps are not detailed so as not to make the document too long.

5.2 Phase 2: Selection of Algorithms

One way to perform the classification of anomalies in DoS attacks is known as Machine Learning; which is able to learn without being explicitly programmed, thanks to a massive set of data (Dataset) that allows training an algorithm designed for the detection of intruders, allowing a work network to remain alert about possible threats. In the last decade, Machine Learning has been used in three fields of computer security [22]:

- In intrusion detection, helping to identify known and unknown attack patterns.
- In malware analysis, identifying polymorphic and metamorphic malware which cannot be detected by traditional rules-based algorithms.
- In detection of phishing and spam, reducing the waste of time and the potential danger caused by spam emails.

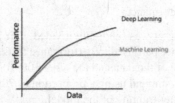

Fig. 5. Machine learning vs deep learning. Adapted from [22]

Although Machine Learning seems to be a promising approach in various cybersecurity problems, it has several drawbacks. One of them is that Machine Learning could incorrectly classify a data packet as non-malicious, accept it for learning, which leads to total algorithm corruption, and subsequently accept malicious packets as benign packets. A second drawback is the large number of packets that travels through the network and that for Machine Learning represents a high level of processing, hinders real-time analysis and could affect the performance of the computer system. Faced with the need to improve machine learning techniques in intrusion detection, AI experts see deep learning as a subarea of Machine Learning, the solution to these problems. Figure 5 shows how the performance of Deep Learning algorithms is proportional to the amount of data processed, compared to Machine Learning algorithms, which over time stabilizes [22].

Deep Learning presents many improvements in intrusion detection over Machine Learning in [22]:

- *Size*: Deep Learning works much better when given a large amount of data (millions), compared to Machine Learning which works best with Low Data Dataset.
- *Time*: Deep Learning requires more time for learning, but this is compensated in its production and operation stage in real time.
- *Dedication*: Deep Learning chooses the characteristics (inputs) by itself and it is the security expert who interprets the results from their approach. Compared to Machine Learning that requires the definition of its characteristics and its labels (outputs).

In recent years, Deep Learning has been used in the identification of denial of service attacks, achieving an excellent classification of packets with different types of denial of service attacks.

Selection of Algorithms. For the selection of deep learning algorithms most suitable for DoS detection, four criteria were taken into account, which are numbered in Table 5. If an algorithm meets the four selection criteria, it is considered a suitable algorithm for the training of the proposed models.

Table 5. Selection criteria

Nro.	Selection criteria
1	The algorithm is available in the Java Deep Learning library
2	The training settings of the model that were used with the algorithm are available
3	The Dataset used in conjunction with the DL algorithm to train the model contains denial-of-service packets
4	The Accuracy of the model trained with the Deep Learning algorithm is greater than 90%

The Table 6 details the relationship between the Deep Learning algorithms for DoS reported in the literature and the criteria that were defined for selection.

Table 6. Application of selection criteria to DL Algorithms

Nro. Criteria / Algorithm	1	2	3	4	Adequate
Recurrent Neural Network	✓	✓	✓	✓	✓
Convolutional Neural Network	✓	X	✓	✓	
Stacked RNN	X	X	X	X	
Long short Term Memory	✓	✓	✓	✓	✓
Deep Radial Intelligence	X	X	✓	✓	
Genetic Algorithm (IGA) y Simulated Annealing (SAA)	X	X	✓	✓	
VCNN/FNN	X	X	✓	✓	
Deep Belief Network	✓	X	✓	✓	
Gradient Recurrent Unit	X	X	X	X	
Deep Feed Forward	✓	✓	✓	✓	✓
(Bidireccional Gradient Recurrent Unit)BGRU + MLP	X	X	✓	✓	
Restricted Boltzman Machine	X	X	✓	X	
CNN + LSTM	X	X	X	✓	
AutoEncoders	X	X	✓	✓	
Deep Defense(CNN, RNN, LSTM, GRU	X	X	✓	✓	

Table 7 describes the different metrics, result of replicated and trained the Deep Feed Forward models and the combined model of Recurrent Neural Network and Long Short Term Memory with the NSL-KDD Dataset as reported in the bibliographic references.

Table 7. Algorithm performance

Algorithm	Accuracy	Precision	Recall	F1Score
Deep feed forward	0.9	0.9353	0.9579	0.9464
RNN y LSTM	0.9555	0.9824	0.9222	0.9513

Although model training with the RNN and LSTM algorithms was replicated with the NSLKDD Dataset, these could not be used to train the new models. This is because the DL4J library required Dataset be already organized, without the need for the pre-processing stage, i.e. the RNN and LSTM methods in the java library, did not contain the method to receive preprocessed data, but required that the Dataset already be with the corresponding features, balanced and with the corresponding label. Therefore, it was discarded because it exceeds the initial objective of the research, contrary to the algorithm with the Deep Feed Forward method that all preprocessing could be done with the DL4J library.

From this process, it is highlighted that the most suitable Deep Learning algorithms to train models that allow the identification of DoS attacks are: Deep Feed Forward,

Recurrent Neural Network and Long Short Term Memory, according to: the systematic review of the literature. Especially for the accuracy performance obtained when replicating the models with the Dataset used by the authors who published the research. In addition, they meet the selection criteria. For technical specifications, of these three algorithms, the Deep Feed Forward algorithm was chosen, which when trained with the CICDDOS2019 Dataset presented an adequate behavior for the detection of DoS attacks.

5.3 Phase 3: Building Classification Models

The Table 8 details the performance obtained from the training of the different models, using the selected Deep Feed Forward algorithm and the selected CicdDoS2019 Dataset, changing the configuration of hyper parameters for each model presented in phase 3 of the Methodology.

Table 8. Performance of implemented models

Model No.	Features	Labels	Accuracy	Precision	Recall	F1 Score
1	22	13	0,6557	0,7212	0,6359	0,6623
2	22	13	0,3225	0,2974	0,3101	0,3598
3	22	13	0,4256	0,4618	0,4059	0,4233
4	22	13	0,6106	0,6329	0,5894	0,558
5	22	13	0,5679	0,6369	0,5416	0,5097
6	22	13	0,5971	0,6781	0,5753	0,5906
7	22	13	0,595	0,569	0,5814	0,5279
8	22	13	0,5736	0,5494	0,5512	0,5694
9	22	13	0,5795	0,6228	0,5487	0,5192
10	22	13	0,6409	0,6509	0,6309	0,5739
11	22	13	0,3816	0,4722	0,3603	0,285
12	22	13	0,6529	0,6929	0,6538	0,6303
13	22	13	0,6456	0,7022	0,6458	0,6731
14	22	13	0,6455	0,6926	0,6622	0,6204
15	22	13	0,6524	0,7815	0,6397	0,6037
16	22	13	0,6566	0,69	0,6509	0,6865
17	22	13	0,2036	0,2832	0,1826	0,1988
18	22	13	0,2766	0,4002	0,3026	0,3154
19	22	13	0,3556	0,2527	0,3144	0,2556
20	22	13	0,3138	0,3696	0,327	0,3077
21	22	13	0,4807	0,4942	0,4455	0,4558

(continued)

Table 8. (*continued*)

Model No.	Features	Labels	Accuracy	Precision	Recall	F1 Score
22	22	13	0,7293	0,8012	0,6721	0,7794
23	22	13	0,3123	0,2527	0,3144	0,2556
24	22	13	0,3949	0,4244	0,4025	0,3599
25	73	13	0,4215	0,3684	0,4182	0,3468
26	73	13	0,3151	0,3449	0,3268	0,2859
27	73	13	0,638	0,6854	0,6494	0,6022
28	73	13	0,6457	0,6891	0,6586	0,6143

The accuracy highlighted in the Table 8 corresponds to the trained model with the best Accuracy: the No.22 model with 13 classification labels (12 DoS attacks and benign). The Fig. 6 illustrates the performance of model No.22.

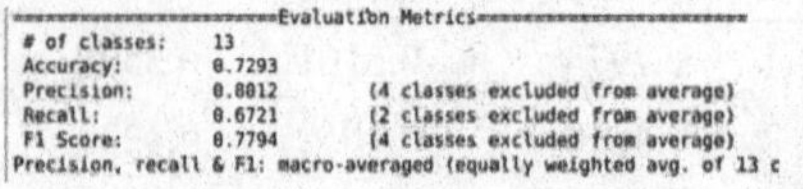

Fig. 6. Results of model evaluation No. 22 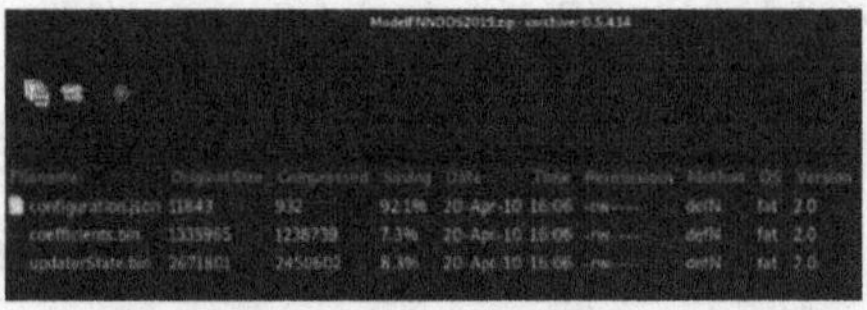   **Fig. 7.** Trained model binary file

Trained models are stored in a compressed zip file, which contains three files: two.bin; one contains the model configuration and the other contains the model weights. The third file has the neural network configuration in Json format. The Fig. 7 shows the files for each trained model.

The trained model performed at Accuracy of 0.7293, Precision of 0.8012, Recall 0.6721 and F1 Score of 0.7794. In the scientific literature the model most approximates to the one created in this research is the thirteen-class model (12 DoS attacks and 1 benign) developed by the same creators of the CICDDOS2019 Dataset, which obtained a Precision of 0.78, Recall 0.65 and F1 score of 0.69 [18]. In this work they used Machine Learning techniques, which allows to verify the best behavior of Deep Learning with respect to Machine Learning in the detection of DoS attacks.

6   Conclusions and Future Work

Given the complexity characteristics of denial-of-service attacks, we recommend that you use anomaly-based intrusion detection techniques instead of signature-based ones. The artificial intelligence networking technique that presents a better behavior in the detection of intrusions is Deep Learning. The most suitable Deep Learning algorithms for training models for the identification of DoS attacks are Deep Feed Forward, Recurrent Neural Network and Long Short Term Memory. Of these three algorithms, this research selected the Deep Feed Forward algorithm, which when trained with the CICDDOS2019

Dataset, obtained accuracy performance of 0.7293, Precision of 0.8012, Recall 0.6721 and F1 Score of 0.7794 for the classification model of 13 classes (12 DoS attacks and 1 benign). Which are very promising metrics, despite the hardware resource limitations that the research was developed, improving this condition is one of the future tasks. The model reported in the scientific literature that is closest to the one used in this research is that of the Canadian cybersecurity institute, which uses an algorithm with the Deep Feed Forward neural network. With the NSL-KDD dataset, which has thirteen classes (12 DoS and Benign), the best report obtained is a precision of 0.78, a recovery of 0.65 and an F1 score of 0.69 [18]. In this work, they use Machine Learning techniques, which allows to verify the best behavior of Deep Learning with respect to Machine Learning in the detection of DoS attacks.

As future work, it is proposed to deepen this research on the implementation of Deep Learning for the detection of DoS attacks as follows:

- To implement the algorithm obtained in a computer system with a controlled environment to validate its operation.
- To optimize the Deep Learning algorithm, based on Deep Feed Forward in order to improve performance for the recognition of DoS attacks.
- To improve the training of classification models, so the model could rank with a higher percentage. One possibility is to adapt the model so that it only recognizes whether an attack occurs or not, since the important thing is to prevent the attack and not so much to identify what type of attack is being suffered.
- Extend the CICDDOS2019 Dataset, allowing for more data and recognition of other DoS attacks, to improve training models.

References

1. Sungur Unal, A., Hacibeyoglu, H.: Detection of DDOS attacks in network traffic using deep learning. In: International Conference on Advanced Technologies, Computer Engineering and Science (ICATCES 2018) (2018)
2. Ahlgren, M.: websitehostingrating, 23 Marzo 2021. https://www.websitehostingrating.com/es/cybersecurity-statistics-facts/#cybersecurity-statistics
3. Alom, M.Z., Taha, T.M.: Network intrusion detection for cyber security using unsupervised deep learning approaches. Dep. Electr. Comput. Eng., 63–69 (2017)
4. Amarasinghe, K., Kenney, K., Manic, M.: Toward explainable deep neural network based anomaly detection. In: 2018 11th International Conference on Human System Interaction (HSI) (2018)
5. Amma, N.G., Subramanian, S.: VCDeepFL vector convolutional deep feature learning approach for identification of known and unknown denial of service attacks. In: TENCON 2018-2018 IEEE Region 10 Conference (2018)
6. Apruzzese, G., Colajanni, M., Ferretti, L., Guido, A., Marchetti, M.: On the effectiveness of machine and deep learning for cyber security. In: 10th International Conference on Cyber Conflict (2018)
7. Barik, K., Priyadarshini, R.: A deep learning based intelligent framework to mitigate DDoS attack in fog environment. J. King Saud Univ. Comput. Inf. Sci. (2019)

8. Chiba, Z., Abghour, N., Moussaid, K., omri, A.E., Rida, M.: Intelligent approach to build a deep neural network based IDS for cloud environment using combination of machine learning algorithms. Comput. Secur., **86**, 291–317 (2019)

9. Chockwanich, N., Visoottiviseth, V.: Intrusion detection by deep learning with tensorflow. In: 2019 21st International Conference on Advanced Communication Technology (ICACT) (2019)

10. Computerworld.: Computerworld. https://computerworld.co/aumentan-ataques-de-denega cion-de-servicios/. Accessed 11 July 2020

11. Imamverdiyev, Y., Abdullayeva, F.: Deep Learning Method for Denial of Service Attack Detection Based on Restricted Boltzmann Machine. Research Gate (2018)

12. Islam, A.A.: Detection of various denial of service and distributed denial. In: Proceedings of 2009 12th International Conference on Computer and Information Technology, Dhaka, Bangladesh, pp. 603–607. ICCIT 2009 (2009)

13. Kasongo, S.M., Sun, Y.: A deep long short-term memory based classifier for wireless intrusion detection system. ICT Express **6**, 98–103 (2019)

14. Khuphiran, P., Leelaprute, P., Uthayopas, P., Ichikawa, K., Watanakeesunt, W.: Performance comparison of machine learning models for DDoS attacks detection. In: 2018 22nd International Computer Science and Engineering Conference (ICSEC) (2018)

15. Kim, T.-Y., Cho, S.-B.: Web traffic anomaly detection using C-LSTM neural networks. Expert Syst. Appl. **106**, 66–76 (2018)

16. Liu, H., Lang, B., Liu, M., Yanb, H.: CNN and RNN based payload classification methods for attack detection. Knowl. Based Syst. **163**, 322–341 (2019)

17. Bhuvaneswari Amma, N.G., Selvakumar, S.: Deep radial intelligence with cumulative incarnation approach for detecting denial of service attacks. Neurocomputing **340**, 294–308 (2019)

18. Sharafaldin, I., Lashkari, A.H., Hakak, S., Ghorbani, A.A.: Developing realistic distributed denial of service (DDoS) attack dataset and taxonomy (2019)

19. Siracusano, M., Shiales, S., Ghita, B.: Detection of LDDoS attacks based on TCP connection parameters. In: Global Information Infraestructure and Networking Symposium, vol. 6 (2018)

20. Thilina, A., et al.: Intruder detection using deep learning and association rule mining. In: IEEE International Conference on Computer and Information Technology (2016)

21. Yuan, X., C. Li: DeepDefense identifying DDoS attack via deep learning. In: Large-Scale Intelligent Systems Laboratory (2017)

22. Xing, Y., et al.: Machine learning and deep learning methods for cybersecurity. IEEE Access **6**, 35365–35381 (2018)

23. Xu, C., Shen, J., Du, X., Zhang, F.: An Intrusion detection system using a deep neural network with gated recurrent units. IEEE Access **6**, 48697–48707 (2018)

24. Yadav, S., Subramanian, S.: Detection of application layer DDoS attack by feature learning using Stacked AutoEncoder. In: 2016 International Conference on Computational Techniques in Information and Communication Technologies (ICCTICT) (2016)

25. Zargar, S.T., Joshi, J., Tipper, D.: A survey of defense mechanisms against distributed denial of service (DDoS) flooding attacks. IEEE, pp. 2046–2069 (2013)

Correlations and Cross-Correlations in Temperature and Relative Humidity Temporal Series From Manizales, Colombia

Luis Felipe García Arias[1] , Daniel Espinosa[1] , Emilcy Hernández-Leal[2] ,
Luis Ocampo[1], and Néstor Darío Duque-Méndez[1(✉)]

[1] Universidad Nacional de Colombia, Carrera 27 # 64-60, Manizales, Colombia
{lufgarciaar,daespinosag,locampow,ndduqueme}@unal.edu.co
[2] Universidad de Medellín, Carrera 87 # 30-65, Medellín, Colombia
ejhernandezl@udem.edu.co

Abstract. The analysis of air temperature and relative humidity is fundamental in several areas of knowledge. For example, they define the climate, establish the population's development in a region, and be indicators of climate change. Cross-correlation and autocorrelation analysis are well-known tools to characterize data series. However, the traditional statistical methods cannot be appropriately applied to long-term climatological series since they are non-stationary. The Detrended Fluctuation Analysis (DFA) and the Detrended Cross-Correlation Analysis (DCCA) are tools to find relationships within and between non-stationary series. This work analyzes autocorrelations and cross-correlations for relative humidity and air temperature series of four stations in Manizales. First, a windowed detrended fluctuation analysis was applied to the series to identify the yearly persistence of the series. Then, the DFA shows long-term persistence for all the series. Finally, a matrix-based algorithm was implemented to perform the DCCA; this analysis showed negative correlations between the air temperature and relative humidity series, following their physical behavior. Besides, the DCCA analysis showed positive correlations among the humidity series of different stations. Similar results were obtained and among the air temperature series of different locations.

Keywords: Air temperature · Correlations · Cross-correlations ·
Detrended cross-correlation analysis (DCCA) · Detrended fluctuation
analysis (DFA) · Relative humidity

1 Introduction

Air temperature and relative humidity are essential variables in defining the climate of a region. Moreover, they influence economic activities and, in general, the

---

Supported by Universidad Nacional de Colombia.

E. Gonzalez et al. (Eds.): CCC 2021, CCIS 1594, pp. 65–80, 2022.
https://doi.org/10.1007/978-3-031-19951-6_5

development of the population. For instance, Wang et al. [25] described how air temperature and relative humidity impact the transmission of Covid-19, a topic of great interest in today's world. The first general rule of thumb when trying to relate air temperature to relative humidity suggests that with increasing temperature, the air becomes drier; consequently, relative humidity decreases. Conversely, as the temperature decreases, the air becomes more humid; the relative humidity increases [23]. The study of the behavior patterns of air temperature and relative humidity is crucial, given their significant influence in determining the climate of a region.

Manizales is located in the western center of Colombia on the central mountain range of the Andes, in the region known as the "coffee axis". Characterized by high climatic variability, typical of the Andean regions of Colombia in both spatial and temporal terms, Manizales is the most populated city and capital of the department of Caldas. Climate analysis processes are taking more relevance in this region due to their pacification and environmental management of urban areas [5].

This work presents a study of the auto-correlation and cross-correlation in air temperature and relative humidity series of the city of Manizales. Air temperature is a meteorological variable that refers to the degree of specific heat in the air at a given place and time. In other words, this climatic variables indicates the warming or cooling that results from the heat exchange between the atmosphere and the earth. Temperature can be measured under different scales and units; one of the most common is Celcius degrees. Indicators such as maximum, minimum, and average temperature are derived from this variable, characterizing the climate in an environment. In the particular case of Manizales, it is described that the temperature has a short-term variability characteristic of the Andean zone. This means that the city presents very stable patterns, but at the intra-daily level, essential variations can be identified in the amplitude of the temperature throughout the city, and throughout the day [27].

On the other hand, relative humidity represents the relationship between the amount of water vapor contained in the air and the maximum amount that the air would contain at a given temperature. The relative humidity is measured as a percentage, and it fluctuates between 0 (dehydrated air) and 100% (saturated air). Different indicators are calculated from the relative humidity, such as maximum, average, and minimum. Those indicators are associated with precipitation and air temperature and are calculated for specific periods, such as daily, monthly, annually. In Manizales, this variable has a stable behavior, typical of the Andean region and similar to what happens with temperature. Therefore, a bimodal type variable is considered, with two maximum peaks (April–May and November–December) and the two minimum peaks (February–March and July–September) [15].

Air temperature and relative humidity are variables that are also used to explain or obtain other variables associated with weather. The evapotranspiration, for instance, is a defiant variable to be calculated [2] but can be obtained based on air temperature and humidity with the use of machine and deep learning techniques [6]. Furthermore, climate change can be measured by checking air temperature and relative humidity. Several studies recommend monitoring its trend (mainly temperature) for the generation of comprehensive change management plans [27]. In the particular case of Manizales, a recent study found that the trend was slow and positive for the minimum air temperature. In contrast, the increasing trends were not evident in all the evaluated stations for the maximum air temperature, taking into account the period 1981–2010 [17]. This work also mentions the importance of analyzing more extended historical series to identify signs of change and possible effects on the regional climate.

This paper analyzes long-term auto-correlations and cross-correlations for the time series of air temperature and relative humidity recorded during the 2012–2019 period. Data from four weather stations in the city were analyzed to understand these variables in Manizales better. Detrended Fluctuation Analysis (DFA) and Detrended Cross-Correlation Analysis (DCCA) have been used, this two methods are used to analyze non-stationary time series and with positive results in climatic series [1].

The rest of this document is structured as follows; in Sect. 2, the data and methodology are presented, including the time series description, the DFA and DCCA techniques. Section 3 shows the results and the discussion generated from these and the objective that guided the study. Finally, Sect. 4 closes with the conclusions and approach to future work.

2   Data and Methodology

2.1   Data

For this work, data from four meteorological monitoring stations located in Manizales is used. The data interval used goes from 01-01-2011 to 05-17-2019 for all the stations. These stations are managed by the Caldas Environmental Monitoring System (SIMAC, by its acronym in Spanish), and their data is stored in the Caldas Environmental Indicators and Data Center (CDIAC, by its acronym in Spanish) [4]. Air temperature and relative humidity data were selected from the Alcázares, Chec Uribe, Milán Planta Niza, and Bosques del Norte stations, located as shown in Fig. 1, Table 1.

Table 1. Summary of stations included in this study.

Station name	Altitude (m)	Coordinates	Operation start date
Alcázares	2057	5° 3'59.96"N 75° 31'40.8"W	04-2010
Bosques del Norte	2126	5° 4'59.16"N 75° 29'19.32"W	09-2006
Chec Uribe	1940	5° 2'56.76"N 75° 31'54.12"W	04-2011
Milán Planta Niza	2150	5° 3'5.14"N 75° 28'35.52"W	12-2009

Fig. 1. Location of the analyzed stations.

2.2 Exploratory Analysis

For a better understanding of the series, an exploratory analysis was carried out in two parts: a statistical analysis and a frequency analysis. The results of the first are presented in the Tables 2 and 3 and include: mean, standard deviation (SD), variance, and range of values of the series. The second part consisted of a time-frequency analysis using the short-time Fourier transform (STFT). Once it was verified that the frequency components were maintained over time, the fast Fourier transform (FFT) was used to find the highest energy frequency components period.

The exploratory statistical analysis, presented in Tables 2 and 3, was performed for each of the years of the series to show the variability of the variance as the period of analysis changes; this variability justifies the use of long-term methods to analyze the correlation between time series.

The air temperature series for all stations have higher energy frequency components with periods of 8 h, 12 h, one day and 1365 days. In addition, the energy for each component is similar between Alcazares and Chec - Uribe and Bosques del Norte and Milano - Planta Niza. The relative humidity series presents higher energy frequency components with 8 h, 12 h, one day, and 910 days. Although components with longer periods would be expected, it is not possible to identify them with the amount of available data and the sampling frequency of the sensors.

Table 2. Statistics analysis for the humidity series

Year		2011	2012	2013	2014	2015	2016	2017	2018	2019
Alcázares	Variance	75.52	71.63	72.42	87.44	109.95	87.04	71.12	70.79	80.29
	Average	85.76	84.32	84.88	93.97	81.76	82.72	85.58	85.34	84.01
	SD	8.69	8.46	8.51	9.35	10.49	9.33	8.43	8.41	8.96
	Range	46–100	49–98	43–98	36 - 99	36–99	42–98	42–98	44–98	44–97
Bosques del norte	Variance	72.05	85.7	85.63	106.46	127.06	90.35	84.71	83.83	93.22
	Average	90.92	89.72	89.15	87.9	86.26	86.49	87.87	88.78	88.65
	SD	8.49	9.26	9.25	10.32	11.27	9.51	9.2	9.16	9.66
	Range	44–99	42–100	46–100	32–100	35–100	37–98.56	38–99	42–99	43 -99
Chec Uribe	Variance	76.84	68.6	69.43	86.25	107.4	88.57	67.83	64.2	68.8
	Average	85.67	83.69	84.69	83.94	81.75	82.8	86.09	86.14	84.52
	SD	8.77	8.28	8.33	9.29	10.36	9.41	8.24	8.01	8.29
	Range	43–99	41–99.05	42–98.48	39–97	36–97	40–98.03	32–98.38	49–99	47.62–98
Milán planta Niza	Variance	61.82	55.03	33.09	47.5	48.46	31.22	27.34	26.91	29.49
	Average	88.03	85.25	83.94	83.02	78.55	79.59	82.11	81.74	79.43
	SD	7.89	7.42	5.75	6.89	6.96	5.59	5.23	5.19	5.43
	Range	48–99	49–96	47–92	37–92	35–87	41–88.07	42–89	47–89	46–87.89

Table 3. Statistics analysis for the temperature series

Year		2011	2012	2013	2014	2015	2016	2017	2018	2019
Alcázares	Variance	4.8	4.5	4.9	5.5	5.9	6.2	4.9	5.3	5.5
	Average	17.2	17.7	18.0	18.7	19.8	20.0	19.0	19.0	19.5
	SD	2.2	2.1	2.2	2.3	2.4	2.5	2.2	2.3	2.4
	Range	12.7–25.1	12.6–25.1	13.3–25.8	14.1–27.6	14.7–28.3	12.5–29.6	14.4–27.4	13.3–27.5	14.7–27.9
Bosques del norte	Variance	5.5	5.8	6.6	6.5	7.2	7.4	6.3	6.3	6.9
	Average	17.2	17.6	17.2	17.01 ± 2.55	17.4	18.2	17.2	17.2	17.6
	SD	2.3	2.4	2.6	2.6	2.7	2.7	2.5	2.5	2.6
	Range	11.8–24.7	12.2–25.33	11.1–24.9	11.6–25.2	10.3–25.8	6.2–26.9	9.7–26.2	11.3–25.8	12.4–26.6
Chec Uribe	Variance	6.0	5.8	6.2	6.7	7.5	8.2	6.1	6.1	6.9
	Average	18.9	19.4	19.5	20.1	20.9	20.9	19.2	19.3	20.0
	SD	2.5	2.4	2.5	2.6	2.7	2.9	2.5	2.5	2.6
	Range	14.1–27.3	13.9–27.7	14.7–27.3	15.0–29.1	15.2–29.7	12.1–30.60	12.9–27.4	14.1–27.6	15.0–28.8
Milán planta Niza	Variance	4.8	4.8	4.7	4.9	5.8	6.1	4.8	5.2	5.8
	Average	16.4	16.8	17.2	18.4	18.9	19.1	18.1	18.0	18.3
	SD	2.2	2.2	2.2	2.2	2.4	2.5	2.2	2.3	2.4
	Range	11.6–23.8	11.7–24.8	12.9–24.5	13.9–26.3	13.4–27.0	11.2–28.1	13.7–26.0	10.9–25.8	12.9–26.5

2.3 Detrended Fluctuation Analysis

One of the methods used to compare the autocorrelation in the time series of air temperature and relative humidity was Detrended Fluctuation Analysis (DFA), initially introduced by [19] and later extended by [10,13]. Additionally, it has been applied in other fields of study such as medicine [3,18], finance [16,24], geophysics [9,14], among others. The Detrended fluctuation Analysis consists of several steps that can be described by Eq. 1. Let be $x(k)$ a non-stationary series of length N to be analyzed using the DFA algorithm. First, the series is integrated to obtain $\hat{x}(k)$. Then, it is divided into s non-overlapping windows, each one composed by n samples of the original series. For each segment, the local trend $(\bar{x}(k))$ is estimated by calculated a least square fit with a chioced order. The detrended series is obtained by subtracting the local trend from each segment. After, the local variance for each segment is computed. Finally, the DFA is calculated as the mean of the local variances.

A power law $F_{DFA}^2(n) \propto n^\alpha$ can be found by repeatedly applying the algorithm for several non-overlapping windows of different sizes. By analyzing the value of α, different conclusions about the nature of the series. According to [1,19]: $\alpha = 0.5$ shows uncorrelated signal, $\alpha > 0.5$ indicates persistent long-term correlations and $\alpha < 0.5$ indicates persistent long-term anti-correlations.

$$F_{DFA}^2(n) = \frac{1}{sn} \sum_{i=1}^{s} \sum_{k=1}^{n} [\hat{\mathbf{x}}(k) - \bar{\mathbf{x}}_i]^2 \tag{1}$$

2.4 Detrended Cross-Correlation Analysis

For two non-stationary time series recorded simultaneously, detrended cross-correlation analysis (DCCA) can be used to analyze power-law cross-correlations. This method was introduced in [22] and later extended in [12,20,21]. In the environmental data series, it has been applied, with temperature and pressure in [11] and air pollution in [26]. There are also jobs in areas such as finance [7,8].

The DCCA consists of several steps that can be described by Eq. 2. Let be $x(k)$ and $y(k)$ two non-stationary series of length N to be analyzed using the DCCA algorithm. First, both series are integrated to obtain $\hat{\mathbf{x}}(k)$ and $\hat{\mathbf{y}}(k)$. Then, they are divided into s non-overlapping windows, each one composed by n samples of the original series. For each segment, the local trend is estimated by calculated a least square fit with a choiced order. Two detrended series are obtained by substracting the local trend from each segment. After, the local co-variance for each segment is founded by computing the hadamard product—the element-wise product of vectors—. Finally, the DCCA is calculated as the mean of the local co-variances.

Similar to the DFA method, a power-law $F_{DCCA}^2(n) \propto n^\lambda$ can be found by repeatedly applying the algorithm for several non-overlapping windows of different sizes. By analyzing the value of λ, different conclusions about the nature of the series can be made. According to [1,20,22]: $\lambda = 0.5$ shows uncorrelated signal, $\lambda > 0.5$ indicates persistent long-term correlations and $\lambda < 0.5$ indicates persistent long-term anti-correlations. The interpretation of λ is analogous to the interpretation of α in DFA. In the Algorithm 1, the pseudocode for the DCCA calculation is presented.

In order to relate the results of DCCA and DFA, one can calculate ρ_{DCCA}. The interpretation of the values of this coefficient is similar to Pearson's correlation: values close to 1 imply positively correlated series, values close to -1 mean negatively correlated series. However, values that oscillate around 0 show that the series are not correlated.

$$F_{DCCA}^2(n) = \frac{1}{sn} \sum_{i=1}^{s} \sum_{k=1}^{n} [\hat{\mathbf{x}}(k) - \bar{\mathbf{x}}_i][\hat{\mathbf{y}}(k) - \bar{\mathbf{y}}_i] \tag{2}$$

Algorithm 1: Algorithm for computing the DCCA

---

inputs : Historical dataset of last n-values of the first station
$X = \{X_1, X_2, ..., X_n\}$, Historical dataset of n-values from the second
station $Y = \{Y_1, Y_2, ..., Y_n\}$, array of m-partitions $P = \{P_1, P_2, ..., P_m\}$,
degree=desired order for the polynomial fit.

output: Array of new dcca values corresponding to each partition p

```
1  begin
2      prev_window ← 0
3      for each window w ϵ W do
4          X_window = {X_{w_1}, X_{w_2},..., X_W}
5          Y_window = {Y_{w_1}, Y_{w_2},..., Y_W}
6          x_trend ← φ
7          y_trend ← φ
8          for each partition p ϵ P do
9              x_trend_poly = LSQ_fit(X_{w,p}, degree)
10             y_trend_poly = LSQ_fit(Y_{w,p}, degree)
11             x_trend ← x_trend ∪ (evaluation of the polynomial trend_poly at
                   value p whit degree D)
12             y_trend ← y_trend ∪ (evaluation of the polynomial trend_poly at
                   value p whit degree D)
13         end

14         x_detrend ← X_window - x_trend
15         y_detrend ← Y_window - y_trend
16         covariances ← hadamard(x_detrend, y_detrend)

17         detrend_covariances ← (1/wm) ∑∑ covariances
18         prev_window ← w
19     end
20 end
```

2.5   Methodology

The variables are measured by the monitoring stations every 5 min and sent in
their original form to a central collection server. Later, they are stored in data
warehouse after applying several processes to clean the data. For this work, the
series was taken from the data warehouse, and a transformation process was
carried out that included three steps: filtering atypical data outside the 99th
percentile, imputation of lost data, and sub-sampling to obtain hourly series.
Additionally, prior to applying the methods and ensuring that seasonality did
not affect the correlation analysis, the normalization of the hourly series was
carried out. Figures 2 and 3 show air temperature behavior and relative humidity
behavior, respectively, for each station.

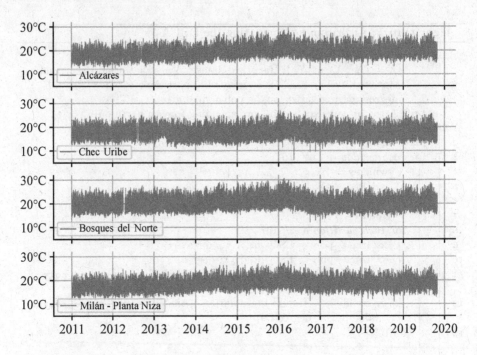

Fig. 2. Behavior of original data of air temperature at the different stations.

3   Results and Discussion

This section presents the results for DFA and DCCA on the time series of relative humidity and air temperature and their discussion.

3.1   DFA

Figure 4 presents the results for DFA for the two variables analyzed in the four stations (4a Alcázares, 4b Chec Urie, 4c Bosques del Norte and 4d Milán Planta Niza). In [1] it was identified that the use of higher degree polynomials in the polynomial approximation does not represent a statistically significant improvement for the DFA analysis in the domain of hydro climatological data. In this sense, for this study, all the experiments were carried out with the simplest polymium (first grade) to minimize the computational cost.

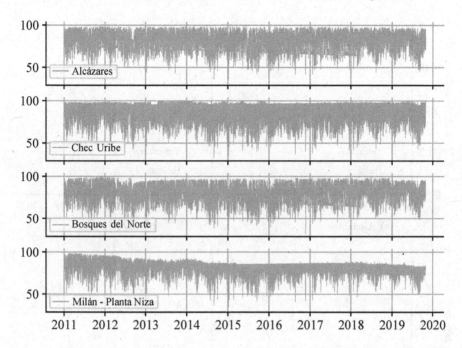

Fig. 3. Behavior of original data of air humidity at the different stations.

The DFA analysis was applied to sliding windows of 365 days with a one-day jump to study the temporal evolution of the scale exponents. Although it is observed that both for relative humidity and air temperature, the power-law auto-correlations are conserved for the analyzed period, the results of the experiments indicate that all the diagnosed time series are far from the theoretical threshold (0.5) of no interpretation.

For the air temperature and humidity series, values between 0.66 and 1.0134 were obtained for the DFA exponent, indicating long-term persistence for all analysis windows. In general, the long-term persistent in the auto-correlation suggests that the previously mentioned variables—for all studied stations—can express their future values as a function of past ones.

The relative humidity time series for the Milán Planta Niza station, presents the highest degree of variability based on the DFA exponent, its minimum is greater than 0.66 and its maximum greater than 1.01 in 2019. Thus, the two variables have similar behavior in terms of variance of the DFA exponent, with a very subtle difference of more significant variability for air temperature.

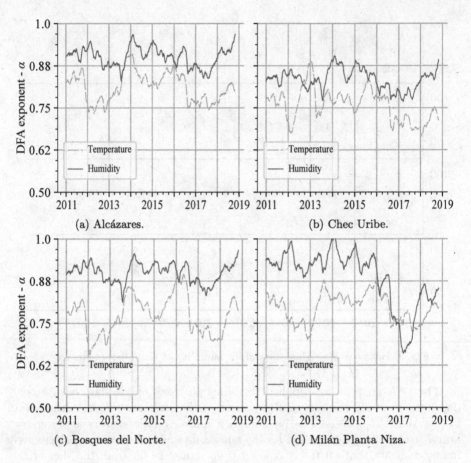

Fig. 4. Windowed DFA for air temperature and humidity series for each weather station.

The relative humidity time series of the Alcázares station, represents the best results in the DFA exponent. In this series, the highest average (0.9011) and the lowest variance (0.0008) are evidenced compared to the other series analyzed. The above indicates that for this station, in the relative humidity series, the long-term relationships are statistically superior for all the analysis windows,taking this into account, the future values can be expressed as a function of the past values with a higher level of significance.

3.2 DCCA

The experiments presented in this section were carried out for a time horizon of 8 years—Sect. 2.1—, twelve (12) analysis windows were defined based on temporal and interpretability—8 h, 12 h, 24 h, 1 week, 2 weeks, 1 month, 2 months, 3 months, 6 months, 8 months, 10 months, 1 year—. In addition, the algorithms for each window were run on eighteen (18) combinations of time series. Firstly, the time series belonging to the same variable between stations—12 combinations—. Secondly, the variables of humidity and air temperature for each particular station - 4 varieties—and finally, the indicator ρ_{DCCA} was calculated for each pair of time series analyzed.

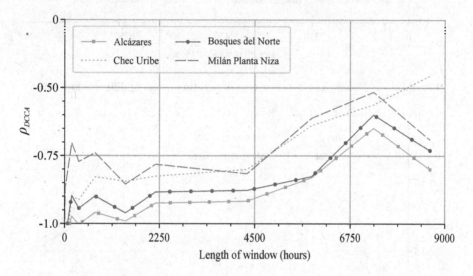

Fig. 5. ρ_{DCCA} coefficient between climatological series of the same station

As a result of the carried out experiments, it was determined that all the indicators ρ_{DCCA} are in the zone that indicates cross-correlation—$\rho_{DCCA} \ll -0.5$ OR $\rho_{DCCA} \gg 0.5$—. Either direct cross-correlation for intra-variable inter-station (Fig. 5) time series analyzes or inversely proportional cross-correlation for inter-variable intra-station (Fig. 6 and Fig. 7) .

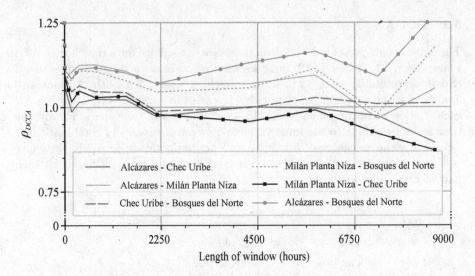

Fig. 6. ρ_{DCCA} coefficient between air temperature series of different stations

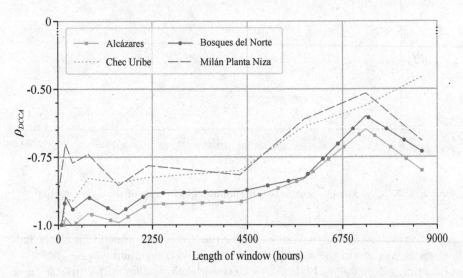

Fig. 7. ρ_{DCCA} coefficient between humidity series of different stations

The ρ_{DCCA} between the pair of variables (air temperature and relative humidity) for each of the stations—Fig. 5—, showed a strong negative correlation—when ρ_{DCCA} is less than -0.5—, that is, the variables are correlated in the opposite direction, this means that high values of one of them usually correspond to low values of the other and vice versa.

The highest average of the ρ_{DCCA} indicator was found in the analysis carried out for the time series of temperature between the Alcázares and Bosques del

Norte stations—ρ_{DCCA} 1.15—, on the contrary, the lowest average of the indicator ρ_{DCCA} was found for the time series of temperature between the Alcázares and Chec Uribe stations—ρ_{DCCA} 1.02—.

The lowest variability is found at the humidity time series between the Alcázares and Milán Planta Niza stations—$\sigma^2 = 0.002$ at the other hand, the highest variability was found in the analysis carried out between, the series temps of temperature and relative humidity for the Chec Uribe station—$\sigma^2 = 0.073$—.

Furthermore, the best representation of the ρ_{DCCA} indicator was found at the relative humidity time series for the Alcázares and Bosques del Norte stations in the eight (8) hour window—$\rho_{DCCA} = 1.46$—. On the other hand, the lower representation of the ρ_{DCCA} indicator was found in the analysis carried out on the temperature variations between the Chec Uribe and Milán Planta Niza stations in the annual window—$\rho_{DCCA} = 0.87$—.

Regarding the window analysis, the lowest variability of the ρ_{DCCA} indicator was found on the daily window—$\sigma^2 = 0.005$—. In addition, it was possible to identify in the tests carried out that the ρ_{DCCA} indicator decreases as the sale increases in size, the window with the highest level of the ρ_{DCCA} was the 8-h window—$\rho_{DCCA} = 1.27$—.

4   Conclusion

In this work, two methods were used for the analysis of non-stationary series, Detrended fluctuation analysis (DFA) and Detrended cross-correlation analysis (DCCA), on the time series of relative humidity and air temperature of four meteorological stations in Manizales, at know: Alcázares, Chec Uribe, Bosques del Norte, Milán Planta Niza. The meteorological stations are located in the urban perimeter of Manizales, and their records are located in the data center and environmental indicators of Caldas (CDIAC). The analysis of DFA by windows showed long-term persistence for all series. On the other hand, correlations were found between the different variables when calculating the coefficient ρ_{DCCA}, which relates DFA and DCCA.

To evaluate the long-term persistence of the time series, the DFA was applied with 365-day sliding windows and 1-day jumps. As a result, values of the DFA exponent between 0.66 and 1.01 were obtained for the all-time series. Furthermore, the results of the coefficient $F_{DFA}^2(n)$ show that their historical values can describe the values of the meteorological variables of relative humidity and air temperature.

The cross-correlation analysis was performed between the humidity and temperature series using the DCCA. A version of the algorithm based on matrix operations was implemented to carry out this analysis as an alternative to the implementations available in the literature and free software repositories. When applying the DCCA method and calculating the ρ coefficient, values were obtained that show anti-correlation, consistent with the physical relationship between humidity and temperature. In addition, the cross-correlation between the humidity series of the different stations was evaluated. The results indicate that the characteristics of the series are influenced by the previous values of the other series and their own. Finally, the cross-correlation between the temperature series of the different stations was verified, and results similar to those mentioned were obtained for the humidity variable.

Apparently, the geographical distance is not influential in relating the time series since the ρ_{DCCA} of the nearby stations seems to be slightly lower in some cases than the value achieved with distant stations. The stations studied were selected to investigate the correlations between the series of humidity and temperature of contiguous and distant locations of the city.

Acknowledgment. We thank the project "Development of a software prototype for the characterization of microclimates and application of precipitation prediction techniques in the city of Manizales through the use of artificial intelligence algorithms" (code 2049288). Also, to hotbed in environmental data analytics from Universidad Nacional de Colombia - Manizales.

References

1. Anjos, P.S.D., Silva, A.S.A.D., Stošić, B., Stošić, T.: Long-term correlations and cross-correlations in wind speed and solar radiation temporal series from Fernando de Noronha Island, Brazil. Phys. A: Stat. Mech. Appl. **424**, 90–96 (2015). https://doi.org/10.1016/J.PHYSA.2015.01.003

2. Castaño, L.F.C.: Estimación y análisis de la evapotranspiración en el municipio de Manizales. Master's thesis, Universidad Nacional de Colombia (2017), https://repositorio.unal.edu.co/handle/unal/60310

3. Castiglioni, P., Parati, G., Faini, A.: Can the detrended fluctuation analysis reveal nonlinear components of heart rate variability. In: Proceedings of the Annual International Conference of the IEEE Engineering in Medicine and Biology Society, EMBS. pp. 6351–6354 (2019). https://doi.org/10.1109/EMBC.2019.8856945

4. de Colombia & CORPOCALDAS, U.N.: Cdiac - centro de datos e indicadores ambientales de caldas (2021)

5. Delgado, V., Zambrano, J., Vélez, J.: The knowledge of the spatial-temporal rainfall patterns as a tool for storm-design. case study: Manizales, Colombia. Authorea Preprints (2020). https://doi.org/10.22541/AU.158921470.04015184

6. Ferreira, L.B., da Cunha, F.F.: New approach to estimate daily reference evapotranspiration based on hourly temperature and relative humidity using machine learning and deep learning. Agri. Water Manag. **234**, 106113 (2020). https://doi.org/10.1016/J.AGWAT.2020.106113

7. Ferreira, P., Kristoufek, L., Pereira, E.J.d.A.L.: DCCA and DMCA correlations of cryptocurrency markets. Phys. A: Stat. Mech. Appl. **545**, 123803 (2020). https://doi.org/10.1016/J.PHYSA.2019.123803

8. Guedes, E., Dionísio, A., Ferreira, P.J., Zebende, G.F.: DCCA cross-correlation in blue-chips companies: a view of the 2008 financial crisis in the eurozone. Phys. A: Stat. Mech. Appl. **479**, 38–47 (2017). https://doi.org/10.1016/J.PHYSA.2017.02.065

9. Hekmatmanesh, A., Wu, H., Motie-Nasrabadi, A., Li, M., Handroos, H.: Combination of discrete wavelet packet transform with detrended fluctuation analysis using customized mother wavelet with the aim of an imagery-motor control interface for an exoskeleton. Multimedia Tools Appl. **78**, 30503–30522 (2019). https://doi.org/10.1007/S11042-019-7695-0, https://link.springer.com/article/10.1007/s11042-019-7695-0

10. Hu, K., Ivanov, P.C., Chen, Z., Carpena, P., Stanley, H.E.: Effect of trends on detrended fluctuation analysis. Phys. Rev. E **64**(1), 011114 (2001). https://doi.org/10.1103/PhysRevE.64.011114, https://journals.aps.org/pre/abstract/10.1103/PhysRevE.64.011114

11. Iqbal, J., Lone, K.J., Hussain, L., Rafique, M.: Detrended cross correlation analysis (dcca) of radon, thoron, temperature and pressure time series data. Phys. Scr. **95**, 085213 (2020). https://doi.org/10.1088/1402-4896/AB9FB1, https://iopscience.iop.org/article/10.1088/1402-4896/ab9fb1, https://iopscience.iop.org/article/10.1088/1402-4896/ab9fb1/meta

12. Jiang, Z.Q., Zhou, W.X.: Multifractal detrending moving-average cross-correlation analysis. Phys. Rev. E **84**(1), 016106 (2011). https://doi.org/10.1103/PhysRevE.84.016106, https://journals.aps.org/pre/abstract/10.1103/PhysRevE.84.016106

13. Kantelhardt, J.W., Koscielny-Bunde, E., Rego, H.H., Havlin, S., Bunde, A.: Detecting long-range correlations with detrended fluctuation analysis. Phys. A: Stat. Mech. Appl. **295**, 441–454 (2001). https://doi.org/10.1016/S0378-4371(01)00144-3

14. Li, J., Zhang, X., Tang, J.: Noise suppression for magnetotelluric using variational mode decomposition and detrended fluctuation analysis. J. Appl. Geophys. **180**, 104127 (2020). https://doi.org/10.1016/J.JAPPGEO.2020.104127

15. López, O.L.O., Upegui, J.J.V.: Análisis climatológico para el departamento de caldas. In: Upegui, J.J.V., Alzate, M.O., Méndez, N.D.D., Zuluaga, B.H.A. (eds.) Entendimiento de Fenómenos Ambientales Mediante Análisis de Datos, pp. 1–66. Universidad Nacional de Colombia, 1 edn. (2015)

16. Miloş, L.R., Haţiegan, C., Miloş, M.C., Barna, F.M., Boţoc, C.: Multifractal Detrended Fluctuation Analysis (MF-DFA) of Stock Market Indexes. Empirical evidence from Seven Central and Eastern European Markets. Sustainability **12**(2), 535 (2020). https://doi.org/10.3390/SU12020535, https://www.mdpi.com/2071-1050/12/2/535/htm, https://www.mdpi.com/2071-1050/12/2/535

17. Ortiz, L.C.C., López, O.L.O., Castro, M.F.A.: Análisis de tendencia de temperatura y precipitación para el departamento de caldas (colombia), mediante wavelets. Ciencia e Ingeniería Neogranadina **31**, 37–52 (2021). https://doi.org/10.18359/RCIN.4900, https://revistas.unimilitar.edu.co/index.php/rcin/article/view/4900

18. Pavlov, A.N., Abdurashitov, A.S., Koronovskii, A.A., Pavlova, O.N., Semyachkina-Glushkovskaya, O.V., Kurths, J.: Detrended fluctuation analysis of cerebrovascular responses to abrupt changes in peripheral arterial pressure in rats. Commun. Nonlin. Sci. Numer. Simul. **85**, 105232 (2020). https://doi.org/10.1016/J.CNSNS.2020.105232

19. Peng, C.K., Buldyrev, S.V., Havlin, S., Simons, M., Stanley, H.E., Goldberger, A.L.: Mosaic organization of DNA nucleotides. Phys. Rev. E **49**, 1685 (1994). https://doi.org/10.1103/PhysRevE.49.1685, https://journals.aps.org/pre/abstract/10.1103/PhysRevE.49.1685

20. Podobnik, B., Wang, D., Horvatic, D., Grosse, I., Stanley, H.E.: Time-lag cross-correlations in collective phenomena. EPL (Europhysics Letters) **90**, 68001 (2010). https://doi.org/10.1209/0295-5075/90/68001, https://iopscience.iop.org/article/10.1209/0295-5075/90/68001, https://iopscience.iop.org/article/10.1209/0295-5075/90/68001/meta

21. Podobnik, B., Jiang, Z.Q., Zhou, W.X., Stanley, H.E.: Statistical tests for power-law cross-correlated processes. Phys. Rev. E **84**, 066118 (2011). https://doi.org/10.1103/PhysRevE.84.066118, https://journals.aps.org/pre/abstract/10.1103/PhysRevE.84.066118

22. Podobnik, B., Stanley, H.E.: Detrended cross-correlation analysis: a new method for analyzing two nonstationary time series. Phys. Rev. Lett. **100**, 084102 (2008). https://doi.org/10.1103/PhysRevLett.100.084102, https://journals.aps.org/prl/abstract/10.1103/PhysRevLett.100.084102

23. Shrestha, A.K., Thapa, A., Gautam, H.: Solar radiation, air temperature, relative humidity, and dew point study: Damak, Jhapa, Nepal. Int. J. Photoenergy **2019** (2019). https://doi.org/10.1155/2019/8369231

24. Teng, Y., Shang, P.: Detrended fluctuation analysis based on higher-order moments of financial time series. Phys. A: Stat. Mech. Appl. **490**, 311–322 (2018). https://doi.org/10.1016/J.PHYSA.2017.08.062

25. Wang, J., Tang, K., Feng, K., Lin, X., Lv, W., Chen, K., Wang, F.: Impact of temperature and relative humidity on the transmission of covid-19: a modelling study in China and the United States. BMJ Open **11**, e043863 (2021). https://doi.org/10.1136/BMJOPEN-2020-043863, https://bmjopen.bmj.com/content/11/2/e043863, https://bmjopen.bmj.com/content/11/2/e043863.abstract

26. Xiang, C., Hao, X., Wang, W., Chen, Z.: Asymmetric MF-DCCA method based on fluctuation conduction and its application in air pollution in Hangzhou. J. Adv. Comput. Intell. Intell. Informat. **23**(5), 823–830 (2019). https://doi.org/10.20965/JACIII.2019.P0823

27. Zambrano, J., Delgado, V., Upegui, J.J.V.: Short-term temperature variability in a tropical Andean city Manizales, Colombia. Revista vínculos **17**, 1–27 (2020). https://doi.org/10.14483/2322939X.17091, https://revistas.udistrital.edu.co/index.php/vinculos/article/view/17091

Educational Informatics

ALPY PLUS - Adaptive Model Oriented to Pathway Planning in Virtual Learning System

Yuranis Henriquez-Nunez[1,2]([✉]) [iD], Carlos Parra[2] [iD],
and Angela Carrillo-Ramos[2] [iD]

[1] Universidad Tecnológica De Bolívar, Cartagena, Colombia
yhenriquez@utb.edu.co
[2] Pontificia Universidad Javeriana, Bogotá, D.C, Colombia
{ca.parraa,angela.carrillo}@javeriana.edu.co

Abstract. This paper presents an adaptive model called ALPY PLUS to enrich the dynamic planning of learning resources with user characteristics and those of her/his context, in order to provide a personalized course in a virtual environment. We describe the proposed architecture, the visual prototype, together with the main components, actions and services required by the adaptive model.

Keywords: Education · ICT · Personalization · Adaptation · Learning pathway · Planner

1 Introduction

Information and Communication Technologies (ICT) have been a means of supporting teaching and learning processes in the educational field. According to Hlib et al. [9], through these tools, the main educational actors (teachers and students) obtain multiple benefits such as improvements in educational practices and student performance in the learning process. According to Foutsitzi et al. [7], ICT enable diversity and availability of online information through digital libraries, virtual laboratories, collaborative tools, and online search engines. Furthermore, UNESCO [20] has stated that ICT have allowed to tackle problems like equality and inclusion in the education sector, by offering people with some type of disability a tailored learning experience in open virtual systems. However, some challenges persist with the use and support of ICT in education, specifically in Virtual Learning Systems (VLS). For example:

– Each person learns in a different way, uses her/his own study method, strategies, and has a different learning pace. Therefore, VLS should consider characteristics of their users, offering a personalized learning experience adjusted to their characteristics and needs.

© Springer Nature Switzerland AG 2022
E. Gonzalez et al. (Eds.): CCC 2021, CCIS 1594, pp. 83–100, 2022.
https://doi.org/10.1007/978-3-031-19951-6_6

- The VLS should support both the learning process for the students and the work of teachers; that is why these systems should not only provide personalized educational resources to their students but also tools for teachers to create material, and guide the learning process of their students.
- Participants in the VLS may have difficulties in handling the interface or the functionalities of the system, which may impede the ease of access and use of the services or educational content that the system can offer.

In order to tackle the challenges previously discussed, we propose a technological solution that takes into account individual and contextual characteristics and the aspects that may influence the interaction of the participant with the system. In this way, we can emphasize on the learning process of the participant, by offering a personalized education adapted to the conditions of the participant in the academic process. This paper presents an adaptive model for *ALPY PLUS*, a learning path planner that covers the topics of computer programming fundamentals in a VLS.

The remainder of this paper is presented as follows. Section 2 describes the state of the art highlighting the conceptual framework and related works with their main characteristics, peculiarities, and ways of use. Section 3 will present ALPY as a general technological solution given the challenges and opportunities identified in Sect. 1 Introduction. In Sect. 4 will be the adaptive model proposed for this paper, providing its profiles, services, architecture, among other aspects. Section 5 presents a prototype to validate the adaptive model for *ALPY PLUS*. Finally, Sect. 6 concludes the paper and discusses perspectives for future work and educational impact.

2   State of the Art

Different authors have approached personalization and adaptation in education from different perspectives. This section presents the main concepts associated with this research, as well as the analysis of related works.

2.1   Main Concepts

The following is a description of some strategies and tools that allow the application of Personalized Education in ICT mediated VLS.

Personalization is considered as the process of change, of adjustment that the system undergoes to respond to the personal needs of the individual, to the person's own characteristics such as basic data, preferences, and interests, excepting contextual characteristics and thus providing a better user experience. According to Reis et al. [18], satisfying the needs and preferences of a person or groups of people is the main objective of personalization in ICT applications. Personalized applications can be implicit or proactive if the personalization is performed automatically by the system. In case it is the user who provides the information or makes choices in the system, personalized applications can be considered explicit or reactive. In both cases, the information system should allow users to have easier access to content and services according to their needs and preferences.

Adaptation is related to personalization, since it refers to consider the characteristics associated with the user and, according to these, the system is reconfigured by increasing the user's relevance in a way that also aims to provide a better user experience. However, adaptation considers both the user's characteristics and the specific characteristics of the context to enrich the system, so that it adjusts or accommodates it according to the user, strengthening the personalization to the user. According to Abech et al. [1], VLS can be enhanced by combining data related to users and exploring their environment, such as location, learning objective, knowledge history and preferences, network infrastructure, and mobile hardware capabilities, among others.

In contrast to the previous concept, in *customization*, it is the user who configures the system to meet her/his needs and/or interests [16]. Customization enables users to take control and make changes to the presentation and functionality of the interface, for example, when they change aspects of the interface such as font style or size, colors, menu commands, both on web and mobile devices. Also, when managing speed dial numbers or organizing contacts on a cell phone, as well as selecting an avatar in a video game.

Recommendation systems (RS) are applied in several areas of user interest such as entertainment, education, health, among others. Their purpose is to suggest options, or the elements titled as items, more appropriate for each user, depending on their interests, personal preferences, and the surrounding context. According to Cena et al. [3] in addition to being systems that produce individualized recommendations, they emerge as a means to help users to make decisions; therefore, an RS should act in a similar way to the way people make decisions, i.e., it should handle a greater amount of information about the user, and it should also consider the different aspects of each individual in the decision-making process.

Planners are systems that allow the user to guide students on their learning path. In other words, it assigns or proposes a set of resources such as contents and activities a course participant according to her/his individual characteristics or conditions. For da-Silva et al. [14], a course can be customized by introducing adaptability in virtual learning systems. For this, it is necessary to consider the learner model or profile and the instructional planning. Addressing this, especially planning, generates sequences of instructions and specific content for each student.

Fig. 1 highlights the concepts mentioned above and the relationship between them. These strategies and tools are useful mechanisms to apply in virtual learning environments. It is important to highlight that it is possible to offer a Personalized Education through ICT by considering a VLS that is subject to all those aspects related to the participant's being. That is, it must connect both contextual pieces of information about the students such as location, environmental and technological aspects, as well as those pieces of information related to the student's profile such as learning style, personal likes, interests. To this purpose, currently popular mechanisms such as the Adaptive Massive Open Online

Course (aMOOC) [8] can be implemented. These systems are equipped to adapt the contents and activities to the characteristics of the users in a course and to customize the system, so that a wide range of learning tools can be easily used in the administration of a course, user management, complements o recommend the most appropriate resources and activities, and route planning according to the educational needs of the user. In the same way, these systems motivate the learning in students through ludic activities, based on pedagogical and didactic models, that guide the design and curricular execution according to the theoretical approaches for learning.

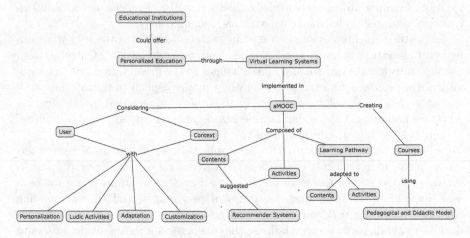

Fig. 1. Main concepts.

2.2   Related Works

In Table 1 each of the strategies and tools useful for applying Personalized Education of the Adaptive and Integral Systems supported in education are presented [2,10–13,15,17,19,21]. It is specified with the box filled in black that aspect or strategy or tool that is considered. It should be noted that most of the works are oriented towards students, followed by teachers and very few towards tutors and parents. As for the strategies, most of the works do not show ludic activities, except for two works that consider aspects such as badges and classification tables. Likewise, most of the works do not evidence the use of customization elements in their systems, except for one work that includes the use of avatars in its interface. With respect to the personalization strategy, most of the papers highlight a wide variety of aspects such as previous knowledge, past performance, student profile, student behavior in the course and student interaction in the system. The resource that is mostly adapted for students is the educational content, followed by the activities, but none of them are personalized. Most of the works reviewed use filtering by contents, followed by activities and one work [11] uses collaborative filtering, except other works that do not establish o evidence any filtering technique or use other technique such as crowd-sourcing or augmented reality. It is important to highlight that all the papers assume that they have a study plan and learning path for their students. However, for these related works, it is identified that most of them do not have personalized learning paths through learning resources (content and activities). Finally, these systems are developed on various platforms, the majority of which are evidenced in a web platform, followed by a development environment with two related works and mobile environments.

For all the above, we identify a need for a technological solution that, in a comprehensive manner, considers each of the strategies and tools mentioned, as well as the characteristics of the participants, their context to suggest the resources and educational activities that best suit student's learning process. Additionally, it should support the teacher's work to generate learning resources, based on students educational needs. The proposed solution is called ALPY and will be described in detail in Sect. 3.

3   ALPY

ALPY is a technological solution that aims to respond to each of the challenges mentioned in Sect. 1, integrating strategies and tools, as well as useful mechanisms to support the teaching-learning process in a VLS. ALPY is the acronym for Adapted Learning Pathway and is oriented to students and teachers in a VLS. It is important to notice that the learning path is unique in the course and the variations are introduced in the adaptation and personalization that are made to the learning resources (contents and activities). ALPY is designed to provide the following features:

– Offer a personalized education adapted to the conditions of the participant in the academic process.
– Facilitate the creation and organization of content in a VLS.
– Recommend content and activities for both students and teachers.
– Manage the activities and contents of the virtual course to generate the student's learning resources and to (re)-plan the activities, and
– Use various ludic strategies to maintain student motivation.

ALPY has three components. First, a database containing the information of the VLS participants, second, an adaptive module that will allow to offer adjustable services in the VLS according to the characteristics of the students and will recommend educational resources to the VLS teachers to be facilitators in the learning process of their students through the learning resources (content and activities). And third, an inference engine based on machine learning techniques, which recalculates rules in the VLS based on established components and adapts according to the behavior of the participants. (See Fig. 2) This paper focuses on the adaptive model that we call ALPY PLUS.This model is detailed in the next section.

Table 1. Related works, Conventions: ✓ Includes appearance, ✗ doesn't include appearance

Criteria		[19]	[11]	[10]	[13]	[12]	[21]	[2]	[15]	[17]
Oriented towards	Students	✓	✓	✗	✓	✗	✓	✓	✓	✗
	Teachers	✗	✓	✗	✓	✓	✗	✗	✓	✓
	Tutors	✗	✗	✗	✗	✓	✗	✗	✗	✗
	Parents	✗	✗	✗	✗	✗	✗	✗	✓	✗
	No evidence	✗	✗	✗	✗	✗	✗	✗	✗	✗
Gamification and ludification activities	Scores	✗	✗	✗	✗	✗	✗	✗	✗	✗
	Badges	✗	✗	✗	✓	✗	✗	✗	✗	✗
	Achievements	✗	✗	✗	✗	✗	✗	✗	✗	✗
	Challenges	✗	✗	✗	✗	✗	✗	✗	✗	✗
	Ratings	✗	✗	✗	✓	✗	✗	✗	✗	✗
	No evidence	✓	✓	✗	✗	✓	✓	✓	✓	✓
Elements for customization	User interface	✗	✗	✗	✗	✗	✗	✗	✗	✗
	Avatar	✗	✗	✗	✗	✗	✗	✗	✓	✗
	No evidence	✓	✓	✗	✓	✓	✓	✗	✓	✓
Data for personalization	Previous knowledge	✗	✗	✗	✓	✓	✓	✗	✗	✗
	Historical perfomance	✗	✓	✗	✗	✗	✗	✗	✗	✗
	Learning outcomes	✓	✗	✗	✗	✗	✗	✗	✗	✗
	Student profile	✗	✗	✗	✓	✗	✓	✗	✗	✓
	Teacher profile	✗	✗	✗	✗	✗	✗	✗	✗	✗
	Student behavior	✓	✗	✗	✗	✗	✗	✗	✓	✗
	Student proficiency level	✗	✗	✗	✗	✗	✗	✗	- ✗	✗
	Student interaction	✗	✗	✗	✗	✓	✗	✗	✗	✗
	Record of activities	✗	✗	✗	✗	✗	✗	✗	✗	✗
	No evidence	✗	✗	✗	✗	✗	✗	✓	✗	✗
Adapted resources	Contents	✓	✓	✓	✗	✓	✓	✓	✗	✓
	Activities	✗	✗	✓	✗	✓	✗	✗	✗	✗
	No evidence	✗	✗	✗	✗	✗	✗	✗	✓	✗
Recommendation system	Contents	✓	✓	✗	✓	✗	✓	✓	✗	✗
	Activities	✗	✗	✗	✗	✗	✗	✗	✗	✗
	Collaborative	✗	✓	✗	✗	✗	✗	✗	✗	✗
	No evidence	✗	✗	✓	✗	✓	✗	✗	✓	✓
Others	Crowdsourcing	✗	✓	✗	✗	✓	✓	✗	✗	✗
	Augmented reallity	✗	✗	✗	✗	✗	✗	✗	✓	✗
Learning pathway	Evidence	✓	✗	✓	✗	✓	✗	✗	✗	✓
	No evidence	✗	✓	✗	✓	✗	✓	✓	✓	✗
Platform	Web	✓	✓	✓	✓	✗	✗	✓	✗	✓
	Mobile	✗	✓	✗	✗	✗	✗	✗	✗	✗
	Development environment	✗	✗	✗	✗	✓	✗	✗	✓	✗
	No evidence	✗	✗	✗	✗	✗	✓	✗	✗	✗

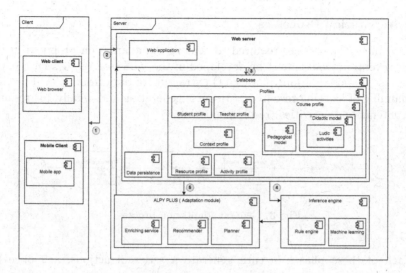

Fig. 2. ALPY architecture

4 ALPY PLUS

ALPY PLUS corresponds to the adaptive model of ALPY and allows to plan and generate a personalized learning resources in a course. ALPY PLUS is designed to accomplish the following tasks:

- To provide the teacher with the necessary tools for the validation of an initial learning resources suggested to the student.
- To provide the student with the individual resources of contents and suggested activities.
- To teach the system to recommend contents and activities automatically, based on the behavior demonstrated by the students and their characteristics defined in the student's profile and context.

It is also necessary to select a platform that allows access to the complete information of the course execution and has the capacity to allow the construction of components on it. ALPY PLUS is composed by three sub-modules. The first one is the *enrichment* of the service; it will allow offering personalized and adapted educational services in the VLS according to the particular characteristics and educational needs defined in the user profiles. In order to achieve this, a second submodule is needed, the *planner*, to manage the resources (contents and activities) of the VLS, and to generate learning resources for each of the students. Finally, the third submodule, the *recommender*, is used to suggest appropriate contents or activities for each student and recommend educational resources to teachers, so that they can be facilitators in the particular learning process of their students through learning resources (see Fig. 2 step 5).

4.1 Adaptation Processes

To implement the services required to achieve the adaptation proposed in this paper, several processes must be developed in the VLS (see Fig. 3). The general process is composed of four phases: (1) extraction of data from defined profiles, (2) planning of learning resources, (3)course generation and, finally, (4) resource (i.e. contents and activities) recommendation.

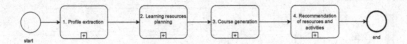

Fig. 3. General adaptation process

Each of these phases in turn generate a series of actions, i.e., once the attributes of the profiles have been extracted through an Academic Management System or in the Learning System itself (see Fig. 4 part a), these data are integrated given the diverse profiles of the students (see Fig. 4 part b). Next, the selection of resources and activities in the system according to the profiles begins, in order to generate the learning resources. Once the learning resources are generated (see Fig. 4 part c), the course is integrated, and the adapted course is generated. Finally, once the adapted course is generated, the student's progress must be verified, in terms of the fulfillment of the learning objectives, considering the resources and activities suggested in the learning pathway (see Fig. 4 part d). If these objectives are not met, the process should be restarted from the data extraction phase.

4.2 Services

The following is a detailed description of the path that a user must develop with respect to the adaptive service in the VLS. According to the architecture proposed for this research (see Fig. 2), among its components, the ALPY PLUS is in charge of defining the profiles and of providing an inference engine that helps in the decision making of the adaptive services. ALPY PLUS also has a recommender system that suggests the resources (contents and activities) for the learning pathway for each student, providing the following services: Generate a particular learning resource, Recommend an activity or content and Planning activities for a student.

The path taken by a student begins by accessing the system through a browser that can be desktop or mobile. Secondly, the VLS responds with a tailored interface that is presented in the browser. In this way, the student is able to identify herself/himself in the institution's VLS by filling out the enrollment data. Thirdly, the system analyzes the data to identify the student, characterize her/him, and subsequently group this data in a profile, for example, basic data, academic experience data, data from initial forms that allow to categorize the

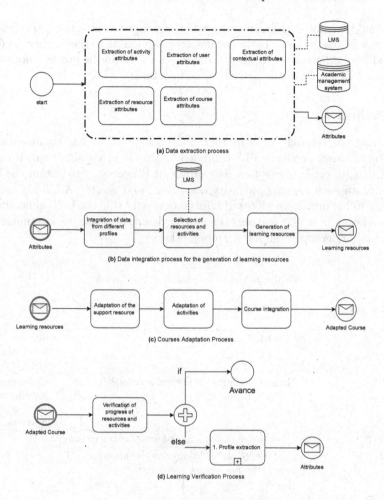

Fig. 4. Specific adaptation processes

student's learning style, likes and interests, data according to her/his environmental context, location or course data, articulating it with the pedagogical and didactic model detailed in Sect. 4.4 of this paper. Once the student is profiled, the fourth step involves the inference engine. ALPY PLUS displays the learning pathway with the most appropriate resources (contents and activities) taking into account the student's characteristic and those of her/his context.

Finally, the fifth step refers to the adaptive services like recommending educational resources in order to help the student to achieve the educational objectives. Also with these steps, it is possible to offer new enriched services to the student, which allow to continue favoring her/his learning, such as, planning tutoring meeting according to student's schedule are availability.

It should be noted that, in order to offer adaptive services to the teacher, she/he will follow the same path, but data corresponding to the teacher would be analyzed from different sources in the database, to obtain the proper information related to courses, students, activities, and content.

4.3 Profiles

Considering the related works in Sect. 2.2, each variable that could allow the definition of a user profile in VLS compiled in Table 2 is also analyzed. It can be noticed that, in order to create a user profile, it is necessary to obtain the basic common data such as name, identity document, and gender. Additionally, it is necessary to include those pieces of information reflecting the individual characteristics of each user like: learning domain, style or pace to learn, commitments, skills, likes, preferences, interests, among others.

Table 2. Data analysis in related work

Related works	Basic and specific learning variables	Other variables
ALOSI [19]	Knowledge status	System interaction history
SALT [11]	Lesslet performance [difficulty(score)]	Common learning and /or teaching interests
EDUC8 [10]	Knowledge, individual and group characteristics	
RIPPLE [13]	Knowledge status [competencies (mastered, adequate, inadequate)], achievement, commitments	
SMART SPARROW [12]	Knowledge, skills	
AXIS [21]	Student learning data, content evaluation	
TOPOLOR [2]	Knowledge of a specific subject, interaction characteristics [content, activities, social media]	
AHA [15]	Performance, behavior	
ADAPTIVE - VLE [17]	Knowledge mastery	

In Table 3 each of these data or variables of the student profile is presented in a general way. It should be noted that when it is desired to carry out the adaptive model in a specific course. As in this case of study (an academic course in Programming Fundamentals), it is important to detail each one of the Profile data (see Table 4). Considering the detail of these, specific adaptive services can be implemented, and new ones can be offered. For example, if system considers data such as the learning style of a student, it is possible to offer educational resources according to the learning style or, considering preference data such as

Table 3. General student user profile

Basic data	Preferences	Personal likes	Interests	Habits	Hobbies
Date of birth	Career	Area of study	Purpose	Frequency of study	Type
Learning style	Course		Career	Place of study	Events
Previous knowledge	Mode of study				

the way of studying or habits such as study frequency, it would be possible to offer monitoring services in the course. In this adaptive model proposal, it is essential to consider other profiles, such as that of the *teacher*, of the *course*, of the *content*, of the *activities* and of the context or interaction of the system with the student (Table 5). The main reason to have these other profiles associated is that, by detailing their data, it will be possible to strengthen the adaptive services and offer new services, making the learning process more personalized. For instance, by considering in a context profile, data such as location or the use of the timetable, it would be possible to define a tutoring service for the course. Another data could be technological, by considering the access device, such as knowing the type of system or the resolution of this device, an adaptive service could be offered in the educational resources.

4.4   Pedagogic and Didactic Model

For this research proposal, the pedagogical model is based on the conceptualization and classification of the development and social model of Flores [6] and the self-structuring model with constructivist approaches of De Zubiría [4]. Specifically, the pedagogical model proposed in this research is conceived as the guidelines that orient the teaching-learning process in a virtual environment without excluding the external environment of its participants for the integral formation of the human being. It is based on the theoretical perspectives of learning and represents the reality of its participants in the educational process. As for the didactic model, it is a means to achieve the pedagogical model, through methodologies, strategies and techniques that allow the scope of teaching and learning. The proposed model focuses on its participants: teachers and students. It is from the interaction between its participants, between their information, the information of the course and between the technological and communication resources that the construction of a relevant, active, social, constructivist learning is made possible based on the principles of Ausubel focused on meaningful learning, Vygotski from the social learning approach and Piaget focused on constructivist learning.

Table 4. Profiles

Profiles	Basic data	Preferences	Personal likes	Interests	Habits	Hobbies
Student Profile	Date of birth [day, month, year]	Career[name, skills career]	Programming language [type]	Purpose [educational (research), labor]	Type of programming language	Type [sports, video games, music, study]
	Learning style [sensitive or intuitive, visual or verbal, inductive or deductive, active or reflective and sequential or global]	Mode of study [type (individual, group), study material (books, devices, apps)]	Programming environment [License (open source, free, paid), color, format, text, label size]	Career [skills (new, complementary)]	Frequency of study [time of day]	Programming marathons [types]
	Previous knowledge [basic, intermediate, advanced]	Domain language [type, level (basic, intermediate, advanced)]	Compiler [type]	Source repository [Repository (local, virtual)]	Place of study	Programming events [types]
Teacher Profile	Date of birth[day, month, year]	Courses to be taught [modality]	Theme [programming]	Purpose [motivational, occupational]	Frequency viewed course [resources, activities]	Programming events [types]
	Courses Taught [modality]	Activities [types]				
	Resources [types]					
Course profile	Course [code]	Location[region]	Areas of knowledge [units of competence]	Class schedule [day, time]	Access rate [resources, activities]	
	Professional competencies [competency units, assessment criteria]	Course navigation [web, mobile]				
	Activities [types]					
	Resources [types]					
Content profile	Content [Types, level, conditions]	Bibliography to consult	Support resource [Types]	Class schedule [day, time]		
Activities profile	Type of activity [level, conditions]	Bibliography to consult	Support resource [Types]	Class schedule [day, time]		

Table 5. Context profile

Temporal space	Environmental	Social	Regulatory	Technological	Structural
Location [Country, city]	Luminosity	Cultural [origin, restrictions]	Law 1581 of 2012 - Data protection	Network [bandwidth, type]	Internet connection quality
Temporal [date, time of LMS connection]	Ergonomics	Economic [purchasing power]	University internal regulations	Device [Type, operating system, screen resolution, browser type]	Network range area
	Noise				Connection application performance
	Humidity				
	Temperature				

5 Prototype and Test Scenario

This section introduces the graphical user interface (GUI) proposed for ALPY PLUS and lists several validation scenarios.

5.1 Prototype

Fig. 5 presents the ALPY PLUS visualization for a Fundamentals of Programming course student using both a web client and a mobile client.

Web client   Mobile client

Fig. 5. General prototype in ALPY PLUS. Student view

In the web client, there are four main services at the top of the screen: (1) *My profile*, where you can adjust your personal data, (2) *My Courses*, which allows you to enter the courses enrolled in your career, but also those in which you are interested, and which are offered in your educational institution, (3) *My Progress* will show the status of the student in terms of the fulfillment of the educational objectives of the topics proposed in the course, and (4) *Teacher*, where the student can find the details such as email and contact information of the teacher associated with the course. At the bottom of the screen, on the left side, there are adaptive services enriched according to the student's captured data, through an initial questionnaire offered the first time she/he enters the VLS.

In the middle of the screen, the topics of the course will be shown one by one. Each topic will be activated according to the accomplishments of the educational objectives. In the same way, the interface also shows the student's own learning path using support materials such as specific contents and activities tailored for each student. Finally, on the right side, all the online users of the course are shown. These users can be either fellow students or teachers. Fig. 5 also illustrates reports regarding the grades of the programmed activities and the badges or achievements of the course. Additionally, in this space there is also a ranking table with student's standings regarding the ludic activities of the course. Finally, Fig. 5 also proposes a GUI for a mobile device (see Mobile Client). Information displayed varies depending on the student, considering their profile characteristics such as their learning style, or depending on their context such as the characteristics of the technological access device, connection performance, among others.

5.2   Test Scenario

In this section, we present a general scenario for the validation of ALPY PLUS. Fig. 6 illustrates the steps followed by a student when entering the VLS for the first time to a course of Fundamentals of Programming. As a first step, the student must answer an initial form that will allow the characterization and integration of their data into the group profile. Next, the student enters the course and is presented with the learning pathway in terms of topics and scheduled activities. Likewise, for each topic she/he will find its particular learning path through resources like contents and support activities tailored to her/his profile. It is important to highlight that the system must also detect other pieces of information during the interaction of the student. It must determine if she/he likes or dislikes the resources and how she/he is progressing in terms of meeting her/his educational objectives. The latter determines the continuity of the topics in the course, but above all, the replanning of the learning resources, analyzing the profile again and giving the recommendation of the appropriate content and activities to the student.

Table 6 presents two examples of data grouping, given the different profiles that can be developed according to the combinations of learning styles from Felder - Silverman model [5], levels of previous knowledge, the geolocation of the student at the time of interacting with the platform, and the type of device used to access the VLS among others. For this particular case, the grouping was done primarily by learning styles.

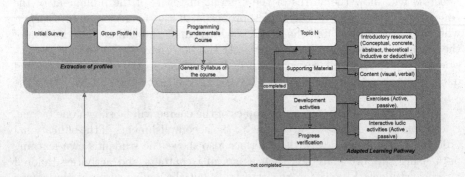

Fig. 6. General test scenario

Table 6. Grouping of profile

Data	Group Profile N	Group Profile N°1	Group Profile N°2
Date of bith	[Day, Month, Year]	10/08/01	10/01/05
Learning style	[Sensitive/Intuitive, Visual/Verbal, Inductive/Deductive, Active/Reflective]	Sensitive-visual	Active
Previous knowledge	[Basic, Intermediate, Advanced]	Advance	Basic
Location	[Country, City]	Bogotá	Cartagena
Temporal	[Date connection]	15/08/21	15/08/21
Device	[Type, Resolution screen]	Web-HD	Mobile-HD

Fig. 7 shows the visualization of the Programming Fundamentals course for the two profiles defined above in the Table 6. It is important to highlight that the course is adapted according to the characteristics obtained for these profiles. To mention some of these adaptive services were the type and resolution of the screen of the access device and the educational resources in relation to the learning styles extracted. Example: For group profile N°1, the course is presented in Fig. 7 as a web client, the activities and educational resources according to the sensitive-visual learning style and advanced prior knowledge. And for group profile N°2, the course is presented in Fig. 7 as a mobile client, the activities and educational resources according to the active learning style and basic prior knowledge.

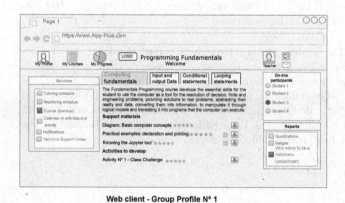

Web client - Group Profile N° 1

Mobile client - Group Profile N° 2

Fig. 7. Prototype according to defined profiles

6   Conclusions and Future Work

This paper presented a proposal for a VLS that uses ALPY PLUS, our adaptation model. The main goal of this work is to face the challenges initially presented in Sect. 1, such as:

- To offer a course through a VLS that considers the characteristics of its students through personalization, as well as the contextual characteristics through adaptation, favoring the learning process of each individual.
- To provide support to teachers using tools integrated in the VLS, so that, according to the defined profile groups, they can suggest specific educational resources through the recommendation system, and validate the learning paths of the students in the course using planners.
- To present a course with a simplified and more intuitive interface that allows participants to easily access and use the services or educational content offered by the VLS.

We are currently at the stage of analyzing the techniques or methodologies to be implemented in each of the stages of development. Regarding ALPY PLUS specifically, we are currently enriching the user and context models, and refining the services and the architecture of the VLS. As a future work, in the short term, we wish to strengthen the rules system used for personalization, adaptation, and recommendation. To achieve this, we plan to define an inference engine and use artificial intelligence techniques. In the long term, we want to implement an Adaptive Massive Open Online Course (aMOOC) to validate the proposal, since so far, no reference has been found of a system that, through a Massive Open Online Course (MOOC), customizes the learning process for its users. Finally, we would also like to develop a module oriented to teachers for defining the learning pathway of the courses and organizing the resources (contents and activities) for each student. All this would be a new challenge whose main advantage is to meet the diversity of profiles that can be generated.

Acknowledgements. The author Yuranis Henriquez Nuñez thanks to MINCIENCIAS, for scholarship received in the "Convocatoria del Fondo de Ciencia, Tecnología e Innovación del Sistema General de Regalías para la conformación de una lista de proyectos elegibles para ser viabilizados, priorizados y aprobados por el OCAD en el marco del Programa de Becas de Excelencia Doctoral del Bicentenario - Corte 1". And Pontificia Universidad Javeriana and the Universidad Tecnológica de Bolívar for the economic support received to pursue a doctoral degree.

References

1. Abech, M., da Costa, C.A., Barbosa, J.L.V., Rigo, S.J., da Rosa Righi, R.: A model for learning objects adaptation in light of mobile and context-aware computing. Pers. Ubiquitous Comput. **20**(2), 167–184 (2016). https://doi.org/10.1007/s00779-016-0902-3, http://link.springer.com/10.1007/s00779-016-0902-3

2. Alamri, A., et al.: An intuitive authoring system for a personalised, social, gamified, visualisation-supporting e-learning System. In: ACM International Conference Proceeding Series, pp. 57–61. Association for Computing Machinery, New York, New York, USA (2018). https://doi.org/10.1145/3234825.3234835

3. Cena, F., Rapp, A., Musto, C., Semeraro, G.: Generating recommendations from multiple data sources: a methodological framework for system design and its application. IEEE Access **8**, 183430–183447 (2020). https://doi.org/10.1109/ACCESS.2020.3028777

4. De Zubiría Samper, J.: Hacia una Pedagogía Dialogante. In: Los Modelos Pedagógicos (2006)

5. Felder, R., Silverman, L.: Learning and teaching styles in engineering education. Eng. Educ. **78**(7), 674–81 (1988). http://www.ncsu.edu/felder-public/ILSpage.html

6. Florez Ochoa, R.: Evaluacion pedagogica y cognicion (2001)

7. Foutsitzi, S., Caridakis, G.: ICT in education: benefits, challenges and new directions. In: 10th International Conference on Information, Intelligence, Systems and Applications, IISA 2019, pp. 1–8. Institute of Electrical and Electronics Engineers Inc. (2019). https://doi.org/10.1109/IISA.2019.8900666

8. Google Trends: Massive Open Online Course, MOOC - Explorar - Google Trends. https://trends.google.es/trends/explore

9. Hlib, P., Zatonatska, T., Liutyi, I.: Utilization of information technologies in higher education. In: 2019 IEEE International Conference on Advanced Trends in Information Theory, ATIT 2019 - Proceedings, pp. 349–354. Institute of Electrical and Electronics Engineers Inc. (2019). https://doi.org/10.1109/ATIT49449.2019.9030449

10. Iatrellis, O., Kameas, A., Fitsilis, P.: EDUC8 pathways: executing self-evolving and personalized intra-organizational educational processes. Evolving Syst. **11**(2), 227–240 (2019). https://doi.org/10.1007/s12530-019-09287-4

11. Karataev, E., Zadorozhny, V.: Adaptive social learning based on crowdsourcing. IEEE Trans. Learn. Technol. **10**(2), 128–139 (2017). https://doi.org/10.1109/TLT.2016.2515097

12. Kasinathan, V., Mustapha, A., Medi, I.: Adaptive learning system for higher learning. In: ICIT 2017–8th International Conference on Information Technology, Proceedings, pp. 960–970. IEEE (2017). https://doi.org/10.1109/ICITECH.2017.8079975

13. Khosravi, H., Sadiq, S., Gasevic, D.: Development and adoption of an adaptive learning system reflections and lessons learned. In: Annual Conference on Innovation and Technology in Computer Science Education, ITiCSE, pp. 58–64. Association for Computing Machinery, New York, NY, USA (2020). https://doi.org/10.1145/3328778.3366900

14. Lopes, R.d.S., Fernandes, M.A.: Adaptative instructional planning using workflow and genetic algorithms. In: 2009 Eighth IEEE/ACIS International Conference on Computer and Information Science, pp. 87–92. IEEE (2009). https://doi.org/10.1109/ICIS.2009.197, http://ieeexplore.ieee.org/document/5223120/

15. Mangina, F., Chiazzese, G., Hasegawa, T.: AHA: ADHD augmented (learning environment). In: Proceedings of 2018 IEEE International Conference on Teaching, Assessment, and Learning for Engineering, TALE 2018, pp. 774–777. Institute of Electrical and Electronics Engineers Inc. (2019). https://doi.org/10.1109/TALE.2018.8615222

16. Marathe, S., Sundar, S.S.: What drives customization? In: Proceedings of the 2011 Annual Conference on Human Factors in Computing Systems - CHI 2011. p. 781. ACM Press, New York (2011). https://doi.org/10.1145/1978942.1979056

17. Meacham, S., Pech, V., Nauck, D.: AdaptiveVLE: an integrated framework for personalized online education using MPS JetBrains domain-specific modeling environment. IEEE Access **8**, 184621–184632 (2020). https://doi.org/10.1109/ACCESS.2020.3029888

18. Reis, J.L., Carvalho, J.A.: Personalization dimensions: a conceptual model for personalized information systems. In: 2014 9th Iberian Conference on Information Systems and Technologies (CISTI), pp. 1–5. IEEE (2014). https://doi.org/10.1109/CISTI.2014.6876933, https://ieeexplore.ieee.org/document/6876933

19. Rosen, Y., et al.: The effects of adaptive learning in a massive open online course on learners' skill development. In: Proceedings of the Fifth Annual ACM Conference on Learning at Scale, pp. 1–8. ACM, New York (2018). https://doi.org/10.1145/3231644.3231651

20. UNESCO: TIC, educación y desarrollo social en América Latina y el Caribe - UNESCO Biblioteca Digital, https://unesdoc.unesco.org/ark:/48223/pf0000262862

21. Williams, J.J., et al.: AXIS. In: Proceedings of the Third (2016) ACM Conference on Learning @ Scale, pp. 379–388. ACM, New York (2016). https://doi.org/10.1145/2876034.2876042

Problem-Based Learning and Virtual Platforms Process in Education for Civil Engineers: An Experiment Carried Out by the University of Medellin, Colombia

Liliana González-Palacio[1]([✉]) [ID], John García-Giraldo[2] [ID], Mario Luna-Del-Risco[2] [ID], and Marta Silvia Tabares[1] [ID]

[1] Universidad EAFIT, Medellín, Colombia
{lgonzalez8,mtabares}@eafit.edu.co
[2] Universidad de Medellín, Medellín, Colombia
{jmgarcia,mluna}@udem.edu.co

Abstract. Materials resistance is the core course for any civil engineer. Historically this course has shown alarming loss rates of 85% per academic semester at the Universidad de Medellin, Colombia. The course is currently taught through lectures and a set of individual tests. However, an improvement plan of the evaluation and learning process is under way based on a radical change in the use of technology, teaching methodology and assessment of progress. Hence, a plan was set up to implement a constructivist approach geared to having students solve work-related problems linked to situations in their professional lives in a collaborative way by means of *Learning Management System* (LMS) type platforms. Throughout 2020, a new strategy was implemented in this course, which incorporated elements of virtual education and active learning elements focused on PBL (Problem-Based Learning). This article explains the implemented methodology and shows some partial results stating advantages and disadvantages. We expect to see a reduction of at least 5% of student loss and desertion. And also promote the use of these new methodologies at other universities with engineering programs. We can conclude that lectures do not promote students' active engagement in their learning process, thus preventing them from acquiring all the skills needed to apply the covered concepts. Being committed to solving a real problem impacts not just motivation, which added to the use of technology will in turn improve student performance results.

Keywords: Problem-based learning · Virtual education · Materials resistance · LMS platforms

1 Introduction

There are many cases that question the efficiency in the design and execution of construction work in the country. Some studies from Los Andes University (Universidad de los Andes in Colombia) revealed that the 2013 collapse of Stage 6 of the Space Building

E. Gonzalez et al. (Eds.): CCC 2021, CCIS 1594, pp. 101–113, 2022.
https://doi.org/10.1007/978-3-031-19951-6_7

(Antioquia) was due to the lack of structural capacity of the columns to support normal loads. Finally, on February 27, 2014, Stage 5 of the building was demolished and the National Professional Council of Engineering (COPNIA for its acronym in Spanish) of Colombia pointed out that the engineers who designed and executed the construction of the building were responsible for this catastrophe. This corroborates the fact that engineering training is critical, and not doing it well leads to disasters such as the aforementioned one. The construction of any engineering work (for example, a bridge, a building, a tunnel, etc.) requires the use of materials that will be subjected throughout their useful life to the action of internal and external forces, which will produce stresses and deformations in its structure. The material stress and deformation values must be calculated appropriately according to its mechanical properties, in order to avoid possible specific failures of the structure and to minimize the probability of collapse throughout its useful life. In this regard, the Materials Resistance Course becomes the cornerstone of any civil engineer.

Historically, this course has reported worrying loss rates of up to 85% per academic semester at the University of Medellin, Colombia (UdeM). These failure rates have led subject-area teachers to seek, together with colleagues from other areas of engineering and education, new options with the intervention of technologies to improve student performance. Another goal is to generate greater student retention of covered subject-related topics, thus ensuring adequate preparation to handle real-life situations that impact many lives.

During the first semester of 2020, an experiment linked to a research project was carried out, in which the selected population were the Materials Resistance Course students at UdeM (University of Medellin). This academic strategy incorporates elements of virtual education and active learning, specifically PBL (Problem-Based Learning).

This course is currently taught under the traditional method of master lecture and a set of individual written evaluations. A course improvement related to the student evaluation process is expected to take place based on a radical change in the teaching methodology and assessment-of-learning process, which includes the implementation of a constructivist approach geared to having students collaboratively solve work-related problems and are linked to the materials resistance area. The above-mentioned initiative is also a good option to promote creativity and innovation, by implementing training processes that stem from the analysis and solution of contextualized problems.

This article shows the design of the experiment, including the applied method, reporting details of each phase with the goal of providing information that allows replicating exercises of this type in other knowledge and application contexts. Partial results of the pilot study are also provided.

This proposal seeks to reduce the loss and dropout percentages and, at the same time, strengthen the competencies of the students who take the above-described subject. The initiative is part of the project entitled "Adaptive Problem-Based-Learning Management Tool to Promote Collaborative Work in Virtual Courses at University Level", research co-financed by Colciencias (call 804-2018) and "Education in Civil Engineering using E-Learning Platforms with Customized Contents" financed by University of Medellin.

After the introduction, this article continues with a theoretical and conceptual framework in which some elements are specified, and the problem is explained. The method used to implement the PBL strategy is then explained in detail followed by the introduction to the experimental design used. Finally, some partial results are shown, as well as the conclusions drawn from the experiment.

2   Theoretical and Conceptual Framework

New teaching and learning methodologies in the field of hard sciences are currently being implemented (engineering falls into this classification). One of the current approaches is Constructivism, which emphasizes the student's active role in meaningful learning, the importance of social interaction in their education, and problem solving in authentic or real contexts [1]. The Materials Resistance Course is an integral part of Civil Engineering academic programs. The subject is part of the area of Structures or Basic Engineering Sciences. The topics offered in this course are cross-curricular to all civil engineering-related areas of knowledge and its main objective is to teach the fundamental concepts and theories on the structural performance and mechanical behavior of the main materials used in the construction of infrastructure works and buildings at the service of society. The course development includes the main physical-mathematical laws developed to date. They explain the mechanical performance of the main materials used by the civil engineer, and at the same time students are trained to be able to interpret all those numerical values obtained from the different mathematical calculations derived from the laws that govern the mechanical performance of materials, and to develop greater sensitivity on the different types of failure of a deformable solid material.

Traditionally, the materials resistance course is taught through master lectures where the teacher explains the properties of materials and demonstrates the formulas that guide their behavior in different scenarios. Students find the subject much more difficult to understand, as they cannot find clear connections to their professional practice. It is in this respect where it makes sense to use active methodologies and the concept of constructivism, which materializes in Problem-Based Learning -PBL-. PBL is an active teaching and learning methodology, the process of which revolves around relevant and meaningful problems for students. These problems are explored in small working groups, the members of which are to arrive at a solution proposal [2]. This teaching approach integrates theory and practice, while facilitating the student's development of skills to solve real problems typically found in their daily professional practice. In PBL, the student must assume an active position in society through significant contributions to the solution of needs [3].

As an alternative to PBL is project-based learning (the acronym of which is the same as -PBL-). The fundamental difference lies in the fact that in project development emphasis is on the conditions of the final product and the effectiveness of the intervention. In both cases, common requirements are the connection that students have with reality and motivational aspects that lead them to undertake creative processes aimed at seeking solutions.

Besides, the teaching-learning process implemented during this course development is mediated by ICT (Information and Communication Technologies), and more specifically by a technological platform [4]. In this type of training, a software generically called virtual education platform LMS (Learning Management System) is used as a means of interaction. LMS have a graphical and intuitive interface. Some of their features include academic management and administration, course organization, calendar, organization of digital materials, activity management, student monitoring, and assessment of learning, among others. Sakai, Moodle, Chamilo, Olat, Kuepa are examples of virtual learning platforms [5].

Seeking to offer customization options on LMS-type platforms, it is necessary to incorporate the concept of learning style, associated with the way students prefer or find it easier to learn. Learning styles according to the Kolb model [6] are classified into four areas: Converger: learning style related to people who have preferences for theoretical aspects and active experimental processes. Assimilator: people in this field prefer learning based on the theoretical knowledge component with reflective experimentation. Accommodator: learning style related to people who have a preference for practical knowledge and active experimentation. And Diverger is the style assigned to people who have a preference for reflective experimental learning combined with pragmatic knowledge. As it was mentioned in the introduction, the materials resistance course (civil engineering) currently has a worrying dropout and failure rate at the University of Medellin. It is necessary to tackle these situations, by analyzing options to improve the rates, and also, develop greater motivation and involvement in students by designing strategies aimed to get students to achieve an active and leading role in their process.

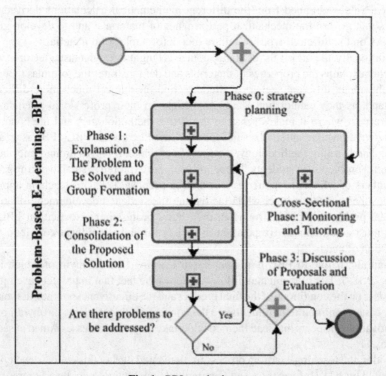

Fig. 1. PBL method stages.

3   Method

The teaching method adopted for this experiment was PBL [7]. Under this methodology, students go from the original statement of the problem to its solution, working collaboratively in small groups. This enables them the possibility of practicing and developing such skills as analysis, writing, synthesis, observation, reflection, a sense of responsibility, and in general, appropriation of attitudes and values, great contributions in their formative process [8]. What follows is a detailed explanation of the approach to each phase (see Fig. 1), as well as the starting point (see Fig. 2), in which the implementation of the strategy and the initial planning of timing, timeline, and other important elements take place.

3.1   Phase 0: Strategic Planning

In this phase, all the general structuring for the implementation of ICT mediated Problem-Based Learning was done [9]. For this purpose, the structures area coordinator (to which the Materials Resistance course belongs) established the conditions of this initiative at

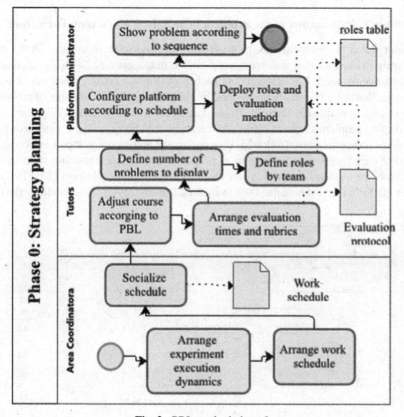

Fig. 2. PBL method phase 0.

management level (Dean, Program Head). He included a general endorsement to develop it, and an admitted assessment percentage of all the work that the students would do in order to solve the problems that would sequentially unfold throughout the semester. The coordinator also drew up a first version of the schedule that was agreed upon with those in charge of the support technology platform, seeking to ensure that needs were met from the technology point of view, but also ensuring that problems would be released in a timely manner so that the students could have sufficient conceptual elements to be able to develop it. Once the work schedule had been defined and socialized, each teacher of the intervened course proceeded to design their course plan according to the requested new changes and the incorporation of problems into the teaching process. All the teachers and the coordinator designed a set of tools and rubrics to be able to evaluate the work [10]. They also defined the number of problems that could be included based on the allotted time and the complexity of each topic. It is worth mentioning that when generating problems for each learning style (a variant included with the aim of offering personalization as per student needs), the tutor also had to disaggregate tasks, maintaining coherence with the type of problem that each team was working on. Another interesting exercise consisted in analyzing the roles that the different team members should assume in order to facilitate group work, and equitably distribute all responsibilities.

3.2   Phase 1: Explanation of the Problem to be Solved and Group Formation

The tutor stated the problem that the students of the course were to solve. A rigorous structuring of the problem was previously carried out, according to the competencies that the students needed to develop, and each problem was broken down into a set of challenges that would be easily understood by the groups [11]. The number of problems was prepared as defined in Phase 0. These statements would be sequentially displayed. Once the first problem had been solved, the second would become visible, and so on until 6 problems were completed (following course content, and grouping topics in a coherent way). For each problem, 4 variants were prepared, one for each learning style. At the same time, the students had to register on the virtual support platform (KUEPA) and answer the Kolb test to determine their individual learning styles. This would be the first

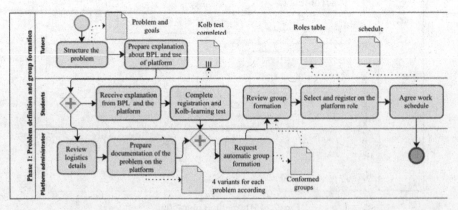

Fig. 3. Explanation phase 1.

input to feed the neural network that would determine team formation, since students with the same learning styles would be grouped together. It is important to note that team formation was randomly done only for the solution to the first problem. In the next 5, the virtual platform was in charge of setting up the groups, through the Artificial Intelligence engine. After this, each member chose their role within the team, seeking to enhance skills, knowledge, assuming a role they were comfortable with and could contribute in a better way. The roles that each student assumed in their team were developed with the support of pedagogical experts and they are not part of the scope of this article [12]. It is also worth mentioning that when the tutors structured the problem, they had to think of variants according to the students' learning styles. Once these activities were sorted out, each team proceeded to plan the work during the time set up for each challenge, and thus the phase ends. Figure 3 shows a graphical summary of the phase.

3.3 Phase 2: Consolidation of the Proposed Solution

As it was previously mentioned, PBL [13] must be implemented as group work. All the students proceeded to organize themselves into small work teams and began to perform the role they assumed in the group, seeking to contribute to the solution of the problem from their strengths. For example, the brain made a general outline to guide all team members on their roles, implementation times, and the best way to address challenges. Meanwhile, the resource researcher searched for the essential concepts and themes in order to help all his classmates solve the assigned problem. At this stage, each group must worry about getting organized to be able to find the solution to the problems within the time frame and the established work schedule.

This is how the workings of each deliverable began, each task according to the active roles, all aligned to achieve the common goal. In the regular follow-up meetings, the team evaluated the progress of each task in order to determine improvement actions in case of delays due to group work-related dynamics [2]. When the deadline date was

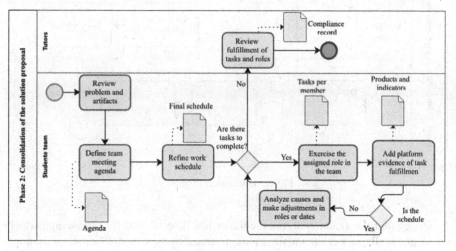

Fig. 4. Consolidation stage 2.

up, the tutor entered the platform to verify and review each deliverable provided by the teams and thus determine if the problem had been solved. Figure 4 shows the detail of the phase as already explained.

3.4　Phase 3: Discussion of Proposals and Evaluation

At the end of the period established for the problem to be solved, the teams deliver an artifact that includes the solution [14]. The delivered artifact depended on the learning style detected. For some it was a pitch-type presentation, for others it was a pre-recorded video, for others, it was a poster. Additionally, each team had to submit a report of maximum 5 pages with a summary of the entire experienced process. With this information, the tutor began to assess the work of each team based on a set of rubrics created and made available for this purpose. The assessment process was carried out from three perspectives: self-evaluation, co-evaluation and tutor evaluation. Figure 5 summarizes the dynamics of this stage.

This stage takes place from the very moment that all interaction between tutors and students begins with the respective team formation. A new role called "facilitator" is incorporated for the follow-up process. The facilitator's main responsibility was to be aware of the questions that came up within the groups with regards to platform management, and problem-solving organization. The facilitator also served as a liaison between students and teachers. This was due to the large number of students per course, which made it difficult for teachers to closely support all groups in solving the assigned problems.

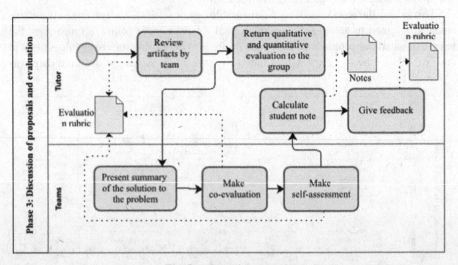

Fig. 5. Discussion stage 3.

Throughout the experiment, the facilitator had time allotted for counseling, which was virtual at all times due to the situations generated by the Covid-19 pandemic, among others. Doubts were also solved on demand, that is, if a group had a specific concern, they could contact the facilitator for advice. In the event that the facilitator did not have enough elements to solve it, the issue was directed to the course teaching staff. As part of the follow-up, the facilitator also participated, together with the tutors, in the evaluation of the groups [10].

4   Experimental Design

The method explained in the previous section was applied to 130 students of the Civil Engineering Materials Resistance Course. Regarding sex, 25.38% are women, and 74.62% are men. Regarding age, the minimum was 19 and the maximum was 31 years old. Groups of 4 to 5 members were formed, using the roles already specified. The selection of the sample responds to a non-probabilistic sampling, the fundamental criterion of which consisted of belonging or not to groups of the Materials Resistance course in the period 2020-01. For the deployed experiment, 6 problems were designed for each learning style, for a total of 24 problems, which were scored by three types of evaluators: students, peers and teachers through a rubric of specifications that allowed standardizing and having an objective measurement of the performance of those being evaluated. In that sense, an evidence-based model was used for the rubric design, which would allow for the construction of waterfall-model specifications, going progressively down to higher levels of detail in each one of the criteria. By way of monitoring the rubric, the percentage of agreement was calculated, which consisted of the quotient of the sum of the agreements among all the evaluators over the maximum possible of the agreements among all the evaluators.

Finally, in order to classify the students to previously designed and classified problems, the K-means method was used because it is very fast and not very demanding regarding machine resources. On a practical level, the classification methods act as indispensable complements of the factorial axis methods, allowing the exploration and description of the structure of the data in a satisfactory manner. This method has two drawbacks: the number of classes and the starting points for those classes have to be provided; and the optimum depends on the initial points, that is, it is a local optimum, which may be far from the global optimum. At the end, the sorting method must classify the problems that will be presented according to the vector of the students' scores and their score vector presented in their learning style obtained from the Kolb test.

5   Results

In this section, some partial results are reported after the experiment is carried out. As mentioned in the method section, one of the first steps was the diagnosis through the Kolb test of each student's learning style. Figure 6 shows the mean and disaggregated standard deviation for each of the learning styles: accommodator, assimilator, converger and diverger. Also for each dimension of the test: *concrete experience, reflexive orientation, abstract conceptualization and active experimentation*. Thus, the group corresponding to students with an accommodating learning style obtained higher scores in concrete experience with a mean of 82.70; the assimilating group in the reflexive orientation dimension reached a mean of 71.19. The convergers presented the lowest mean in the active experimentation dimension with 48.08, and the diverging style presented the lowest mean in the concrete experience score with 56.25. In general, it can be stated that the percentage of agreement consists of the quotient of the sum of the agreements among all the evaluators over the maximum possible of the agreements among all the evaluators and where percentages of agreement greater than 70% and less than the 95% are expected.

Learning Styles	Concrete	Reflexive	Abstract	Active	Sd Concrete	Sd Reflexive	Sd Abstract	Sd Active
accommodating student	82.70	48.17	53.57	65.5	8.40	7.49	8.50	8.82
assimilating student	57.40	71.19	70.98	50.4	12.92	9.03	7.11	11.0
convergent student	80.36	66.39	55.17	48.1	7.21	9.30	9.94	7.52
divergent student	56.25	57.02	67.54	69.2	9.89	7.95	10.28	13.6

Fig. 6. Mean and standard deviation of each dimension of Kolb test disaggregated by learning style.

Figure 7 shows each of the percentages of agreement that indicates the degree of agreement of all the evaluators corresponding to each of the criteria of the rubric. In general, the degree of agreement is higher than 87.81% in all criteria of the rubric, with a mean rating of around 3.53 and a standard deviation between 0.926 and 0.941.

Aspect	% agreement	MEAN	SD	Aspect	% agreement	MEAN	SD
Scientificity	88.1%	3.52	0.936	Completeness	88.2%	3.3	0.941
Clarity	88%	3.52	0.941	Communication	87.8%	3.51	0.931
Originality	88.2%	3.53	0.938	Team work	88.3%	3.53	0.935
Relevance	88.1%	3.52	0.937	Viability	88.1%	3.53	0.926
Results	88.3%	3.53	0.943				

Fig. 7. Disaggregation of the percentage of agreement for each aspect of the qualification rubric

Then, from a hierarchical classification based on a mixed algorithm, which includes the Ward method and K-means grouping, four classes or groups of students corresponding to the four types of learning styles, were identified. Thus, Fig. 8 shows the factorial plane corresponding to students and centroids of each of the problems identified by their learning style. For example, in the case of group 3, the group of students assigned in the second "convergent" type problem is identified in blue and in the center of the group with the figure of a square of a slightly larger size the centroid of the "convergent" problem is located. Group 1 or cluster corresponds to the accommodating learning style, group 2 to the assimilating and group 4 to the divergent style. During the problem classification process, the student was assigned the problem corresponding to his problem with the closest centroid.

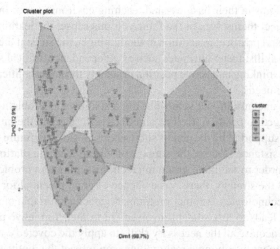

Fig. 8. Factorial plane of individuals and problems corresponding to the second assigned problem.

Figure 9 presents the results for the semester 20191, 20192 and 20201 (period of the application of the PBL strategy). In the graph, it is obvious that the average values for the 20201 semester are comparatively higher with respect to the other two academic periods. The results indicate that the mean of the period 20191 presents an average of 2.30, in 20192 of 1.83 and in 20201 of 3.03 (F = 14.015, p-value < 0.00). In addition, a Tukey HSD test was performed to check which pairs of academic periods present these differences in the final grades. What was found is that there are differences in means between the academic period 20191 vs 20201 and in 20192 vs 20201, both with a p-value < 0.05.

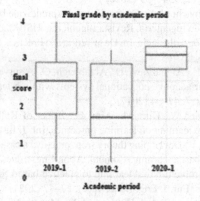

Fig. 9. Boxplot of the mean of the final grade by academic period

6   Conclusions and Future Work

One of the fundamental objectives in the training of professionals is to prepare them to face real problems in their business and teaching environment, or in any area where they wish to project themselves in the future. In this sense, the learning strategies that integrate theory and practice, in addition to facilitating in the student the development of problem-solving skills, foster attributes such as independence, critical sense, innovative and investigative thinking and active position in society through significant contributions to the solution of needs.

Within these unconventional strategies, the one known as Problem-Based Learning (PBL) has managed to position itself as an effective strategy in the university environment, and this is supported by the results shown here. Besides, in future interventions for the Materials Resistance Course, the support of virtual learning platforms will also be incorporated in order to facilitate group interaction scenarios in problem solving. During the design of the strategy, there was evidence of great potential for integrating PBL with the use of technologies. Another preliminary conclusion is that master lecture-type passive learning leads to less student involvement in their formative process, which is why they cannot acquire all the necessary skills to apply the covered concepts. Having a sense of commitment to solving a real problem can impact the motivational factor, and the results can improve. During the co-evaluation carried out by the members of each team, points of improvement were detected, especially from the point of view of raising awareness and not grade well those who did not do the assigned work.

References

1. Keenahan, J., McCrum, D.: Developing interdisciplinary understanding and dialogue between engineering and architectural students: design and evaluation of a problem-based learning module. Eur. J. Eng. Educ. **46**(4), 575–603 (2021)
2. Joshi, A., Desai, P., Tewari, P.: Learning analytics framework for measuring students' performance and teachers' involvement through problem based learning in engineering education. Procedia Comput. Sci. **172**, 954–959 (2020)
3. Castrillón, J.E.P.M., Camacho, J.A., Castro, C.A.C.: Aprendizaje basado en problemas en el camino a la innovación en ingeniería. Revista Ingenierías USBMed **7**, 96–103 (2016)
4. Aretio, L.G.: La educación a distancia. In: De la Teoría a la Práctica. Editorial Ariel, Barcelona (2001)
5. Colchester, K., Hagras, H., Alghazzawi, D., Aldabbagh, G.: A survey of artificial intelligence techniques employed for adaptive educational systems within e-learning platforms. J. Artif. Intell. Soft Comput. Res. **7**, 47–64 (2017)
6. Sudria, I.B.N., Redhana, I.W., Kirna, I., Aini, D.: Effect of Kolb's learning styles under inductive guided-inquiry learning on learning outcomes. Int. J. Instr. **11**(1), 89–102 (2018)
7. Pasandín, A.M., Pérez, I.P.: Developing theory from practice: a case study in civil engineering airport design problem-based learning. Comput. Appl. Eng. Educ. **29**(5), 1112–1131 (2021)
8. Mann, L., et al.: From problem-based learning to practice-based education: a framework for shaping future engineers. Eur. J. Eng. Educ. **46**(1), 27–47 (2021)
9. di Lanzo, J.A., Valentine, A., Sohel, F., Yapp, A.Y., Muparadzi, K.C., Abdelmalek, M.: A review of the uses of virtual reality in engineering education. Comput. Appl. Eng. Educ. **28**(3), 748–763 (2020)

10. Mokhtar, H., Tholibon, D.A., Ismail, N.I.N.: An Analysis of diploma civil engineering students' learning style. Gading J. Soc. Sci. **24**(01), 41–45 (2021)
11. Léger, M.T., Laroche, A.M., Pruneau, D.: Using design thinking to solve a local environmental problem in the context of a university civil engineering course-an intrinsic case study. Glob. J. Eng. Educ. **22**(1), 6–12 (2020)
12. Siemaszko, A., Apollo, M.: Application possibilities of LBN for civil engineering issues. In: MATEC Web of Conferences, vol. 219, pp. 1–8 (2018)
13. Mann, L., et al.: From problem-based learning to practice-based education: a framework for shaping future engineers. Eur. J. Eng. Educ. **46**(1), 27–47 (2021)
14. Yehia, S., Gunn, C.: Enriching the learning experience for civil engineering students through learner-centered teaching. J. Prof. Issues Eng. Educ. Pract. **144**(4), 16–32 (2018)

Information Systems

Cost Estimate Migration for Crystal Reports

José Luis Pulgarín(iD), Félix Ruíz(iD), Camilo Mendoza(iD), and Kelly Garcés(✉)(iD)

Department of Systems and Computing Engineering, School of Engineering,
Universidad de Los Andes, Bogota, Colombia
{jl.pulgarin,fe.ruiz,ca.mendoza968,kj.garces971}@uniandes.edu.co

Abstract. Currently, we are experiencing great advances in various
fields of technology such as hardware and software. These advances
propose various challenges in software engineering in order to face the
maintainability and support of current systems. The cases of software
that become obsoleted by this accelerated process of evolution involves
increasingly complex procedural challenges of migrations and updates.
A clear example are reporting systems which are an essential support
for companies. It is important to build solutions and tools that leverage
efficient migration process. In this paper, we present a model-based approach to cover the migration scenario of reports from Crystal to Oracle
Publisher. The approach relies on three pillars: i) a view with the results
of a function point analysis that aims at facilitating planning task; ii) a
structural view of the reports that allows developers to restructure them
and see the migration progress status; and iii) the actual transformation from Crystal to Publisher. An evaluation of the approach on a real
dataset shows their advantages in term of developers' productivity and
report performance improvements.

Keywords: Model-driven engineering · Migration · Function points ·
Crystal report

1 Introduction

Some private and governmental entities support their business processes on ERP
(Enterprise Resource Planning), CRM (Customer Relationship Management)
and HCM (Human Capital Management) applications built on top of Oracle
Peoplesoft Suite [10]. Peoplesoft modules have been using the CrystalReport
technology to report business operations.

On the second half of 2015, Oracle launched Peoplesoft version 8.55 bringing
with it some bad news: "Oracle will no longer support the use of the Crystal
Reports"[1]. Therefore, if the IT stakeholders of an enterprise want to continue
using the reports functionality, they have to migrate all Crystal reports to BI

---

[1] https://blogs.oracle.com/peopletools/reporting-in-peoplesoft-without-crystal-
reports.

© Springer Nature Switzerland AG 2022
E. Gonzalez et al. (Eds.): CCC 2021, CCIS 1594, pp. 117–132, 2022.
https://doi.org/10.1007/978-3-031-19951-6_8

Publisher (native Oracle reporting module). The estimated cost to migrate all Crystal reports manually is expensive and risky. Each Peoplesoft module has around one thousand reports and most of enterprises do not have developers with BI Publisher experience. This legacy has the following problems [5,8]: i) lack of documentation; ii) lack of hierarchical organization; iii) dead code; and iv) performing the migration manually is tedious and repetitive . These problems make it difficult to determine the scope and cost of a migration in an accurate way. As a result, there may be (over)underestimation of time and budget.

A company brought this problem (see Sect. 1.1) to our research group that has a track on software modernization. Since 2014, our research group has carried out, in cooperation with industry partners, migration projects that used a variety of source technologies (i.e., Oracle Forms, JEE, RoR) [5,9]. These experiences led us to generalize a migration solution by using Model-Driven Engineering (MDE) principles [13]. The cornerstone of this approach is the usage of a Platform Independent Model (PIM) which initial version is obtained from the legacy, and then modified by the developer to target quality attributes. The approach has been tested in both an internal pilot with the industry partners and a pilot with real clients [5]. The evaluation shows that the approach significantly improve developers productivity (around 40%) when compared with the manual migration. In addition, the quality of the new code is significantly higher when following the approach than when applying the manual migration (around 61%).

Even though these motivating results, we realized, from the Crystal Reports challenge, that our approach lacked a mechanism that helps developers forecast migration effort.

This fact motivated us to adapt the generalized approach to provide estimation means for stakeholders to early decide if migration is viable. The estimation is based on function point analysis (see Sect. 3). In addition to this, we fully instantiated the approach in the Crystal Reports case, which resulted in a migration tool that the company could improve to produce business value (see Sect. 4).

The migration tool falls in the category of *white-box* meaning that the approach provides a PIM (obtained from reverse engineering the legacy) and two visualizations (referred to as *Function point view* and *Architecture view*) from which developers can get an overview of the dimension and complexity of each report. This can help them in sizing, prioritizing and planning tasks. In addition, developers can make early architecture decisions at model level before performing the actual transformation from legacy to target technology.

Our approach is susceptible of being applicable to other source 4GL technologies (like Delphi or Visual Basic) because the PIM represents concepts that are common to many report architectures. To reuse this PIM in other 4GL migration scenarios, it is necessary to plug new parsers that create models –conforming to our PIM – from the legacy files.

Besides productivity improvements of the actual transformation, our approach favors maintainability and performance of the reports because we have factorized and optimized routines in the target architecture. Evidence supporting this claim is given in Sect. 5.

The article ends by comparing the approach with the state-of-the-art (Sect. 6), and presenting final thoughts (Sect. 7).

1.1 Case Study

The case study is about a Colombian manufacturing company who uses Peoplesoft. In the company, approximately 60% of digital or physical files generation depends on CrystalReport to operate successfully.

The company has a core business module consisting of 1400 file reports. These reports are defined on Spanish and English languages for supporting multilanguage property. The company uses more than 200 reports by language, for a total of more than 400 reports to be migrated in English and Spanish.

The IT department did an initial estimation of US$9200 if the migration is straightforward. The company also has modules for CRM, HCM and ERP. Therefore, the migration of all modules could quadruple the project budget, thus the company was looking for an approach that helped them to automatize the report migration and estimate the effort. The later was important to the IT department not only to offer the migration service to internal clients but also to external clients as means to diversify the company revenue, taking advantage of their long experience in Crystal reports

Crystal Reports[2] is a Windows-based tool to design, implement and run reports as independent modules or as modules embedded into an enterprise solution, such as Oracle Peoplesoft.

Crystal Reports provides a module to design the report template, there the developer can indicate the Peoplesoft query to populate such a template. Also, Crystal Reports has a report Engine that connects to the database, executes the query, renders data and prints the output on a file.

2 Migration Requirements

Taking into account the company's business interests, we prioritize the following requirements for the desired solution:

- **RQ1:** Migration scope includes master detail reports. The reports must consist of data source and graphical interface definitions of low-middle complexity. These are the characteristics of the reports most commonly found in local companies' systems.
- **RQ2:** It is necessary to ensure that final users' experience is affected as little as possible.
- **RQ3:** Reports performance should improve or at least remain as-is.

---

[2] https://www.crystalreports.com/.

- **RQ4:** There is a need for a pre-migration mechanism that allows developers to make decisions on the reports to be migrated. An example of a decision is to introduce, delete or modify graphical components to display the information that actually matters in the migrated application. Another example is to discard dead code in the migrated application.
- **RQ5:** It is necessary for developers to know the progress of migration, for example, number of reports to be migrated or reports already migrated.
- **RQ6:** It is desired to have a mechanism for the estimations of the migration cost.

3   Function Point Analysis

There is a need for leveraging the cost estimation of migration projects from Crystal Reports to Publisher. To cope with this, we propose the use of Function Point Analysis (FPA) which is a standard method for measuring the functionalities that a program offers to final users [12]. We selected this method to perform the estimation, given that it is a methodology disseminated and tested in software engineering to calculate the size of the software with the special feature that is independent of the technology and which is applicable at any stage of the life of software projects from design to maintenance. We briefly describe the method below. Readers interested in the method details can consult the standard[3]. In the method, the functionalities are classified in the following two groups: *Data functions* and *Transaction functions*. Data functions relate to logic information created, stored and referenced by the application, which is relevant to the user or to the business. In turn, functions that require an interaction with some user or external agents that process data to enter or exit information are called Transaction functions. The FP counting is performed in five steps: i) identifying the boundary of the application subject to measure; ii) identifying the Data Funtions; iii) identifying the Transactions Functions; iv) Determining the number of unadjusted FPs, by summing the contributions of all functions; v) Calculating the final number of FPs, by multiplying the unadjusted FP count for a factor. The factor is obtained by evaluating general characteristics of the technology on top of which applications will run.

3.1   Application Boundary

Because the migration scope of the case study includes reports that do not perform data updates, we count only transaction functions. Transactions functions can be classified in three subcategories: External Inputs (EI), External Outputs (EO), External Queries (EQ). For the case study, we decided to only count EQ because the reports only perform consultations, there are not external inputs/outputs in the reports.

---

[3] http://www.ifpug.org/.

3.2 Identifying the Transactions Functions

To make the count, we evaluate the following elements:

- FTRs: Grouping of data from the user's point of view. For the evaluation of the Crystal reports, a grouping of data is the set of fields of a datasource table.
- DETs: Unique and unrepeatable fields recognized by the user. For this, we examine each field of a datasource table.
- Complexity: We define the complexity of a report taking into account the number of FRTs and DETs. That is, we take the two counts and search for the range of FTRs and DETs in the left table in 1, which has been pre-established in the standard. The intersection of ranges indicates the level of complexity: low, medium or high.

Table 1. Transaction complexity

Transaction complexity				FP by Transaction complexity			
EQ/DETs	1 to 4	5 to 15	16 or more	Complexity	Low	Medium	High
0 a 1 FTR	Low	Low	Medium	EI	3	4	6
2 to 3 FTRs	Low	Medium	High	EO	4	5	7
4 or more FTR	Medium	High	High	EQ	3	4	6

3.3 Determining the Number of Unadjusted FPs

Once the complexity is determined, we select the function points taking into account the right Table in 1. In particular, we check the "EQ" row since the kind of transaction present in the analyzed reports are queries.

3.4 Calculating The Final Number of FPs

It is important to determine the Value of Adjustment Factor (VAF) which is based on general characteristics that rate the functionality of the applications to be migrated. The degree of influence of each characteristic ranges from zero (no influence) to five (strong influence). We have modeled the influence of characteristics for the case study as follows:

- Processing Complexity: it is evaluated according to the number of functions: zero functions correspond to 1 point, a function to 2 points, and more than a function to 4 points.
- Ease of modification : It is evaluated according to the number of groups: one group corresponds to 2 points, two groups to 3 points, and more than two groups to 4 points.

- Performance, Reusability and End -User efficiency characteristics take a constant value of 4 points due to their importance within the requirements of this project.
- The remaining characteristics will have a value of zero points.

Taking the VAF, the next step is the calculation of the complexity processing factor by using the following formula: $ProcessingComplexityFactor = 0.65 + (0.01 \times VAF)$. Where: 0.65 is a constant that indicates an upper and lower limit in the adjustment function. In the same way, the constant 0.01 is a value for adjustment.

Once the complexity factor is calculated, we calculate points of function which are determined by

$$FP = FP_{WithoutAdjustment} \times ProcessingComplexityFactor$$

To clarify the procedure, we will take the INFTRANS report as an example. This report has 12 fields and a single main grouping in such a way that the resulting count is 12 DETs and 1 FTR. With this data, we go to the left Table in 1 and determine that the level of complexity is ranked as Low. To determine the points without adjustment we refer to the right Table in 1 which gives us a value of 3 Points. See the labels highlighted in red in such tables. Once we have this count, we compute the VAF by taking into account the constant values and the special scales of the general characteristics. Processing Complexity has 1 point because the report has zero functions; Ease Of Modification has 2 points because the report has two groups; and finally Performance, Reusability and End-User Efficiency have 4 points as these quality attributes have been pointed out as important in the project requirements.

Adding these values, we found a total of 15 adjustment points (VAF). Finally, we compute the function points by applying the formulas "Processing Complexity Factor" and "Function Points" as follows: i) $ProcessingComplexityFactor = 0.65 + (0.01 \times 15) = 0.8$; ii) $FunctionPoints = 3 \times 0.8 = 2.4$. We obtain a total of 2.4 function points.

4   Migration Tool

Figure 1 gives an overview of our approach that involves the following steps: i) Parsing of Crystal Reports structural information and transformation towards a Platform Independent Model (PIM) [1] that generalizes the concepts of a legacy report; ii) transformation from the PIM to the target technology, which is Oracle BI Publisher for the case study. Note that the approach includes two views on top of the PIM model: i) The function points view that gives an estimation of the migration cost for each source report; ii) The architecture view that presents the input reports and its constituent elements. Developers can use this view to modify the look-and-feel of reports and indicate the migration progress.

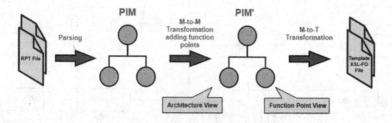

Fig. 1. Migration tool pipeline

4.1 Parsing of Crystal Reports

The first step is to load the information present in each CrystalReport file into a model. To this end, we developed a Java program that: i) loads the file information in memory; ii) creates a PIM model from such an information. The program uses pre-existing libraries that leverages the loading stage. We decided to load the information directly on the PIM to avoid the maintenance of a Platform Specific Model (PSM) and a transformation from PSM to PIM. Figure 2 shows the concepts of our PIM. The *Application* concept represents a functional module of reports such as the Order Management module or Billing module. The *Report* concept corresponds to the Crystal Report abstraction and is composed of three basic elements: Datasource, Page, and Parameters. *Datasource* represents the database fields and groups functions defined in the original file. The *Parameter* element corresponds to the filtering criteria used in the datasource query, and, the *Page* element represents a logical distribution of graphical components (e.g., *Text*, *Images*, etc.) that render the data. Additionally, there exists two control elements: i) the *FunctionalPoint* concept holds the functional point value calculated to a specific report; and ii) the *MigrationStatus* allows developers to keep track of the migration process of each report by using different states, for example: i) A *new* report included in the migration pipeline; ii) A report *in process* of adjustment prior to the model-to-text transformation execution; and iii) A report that contains *errors* that hinders a straightforward migration.

These abstractions tackle four different concerns which are in line with the project requirements: i) the data-source information needed to represent master-detail reports of complexity that ranges from low to middle (RQ1); ii) the graphical disposition of the reports (RQ2 and RQ4); iii) the migration status (RQ5); and iv) the function points analysis results (RQ6). We have marked the meta-model with different kind of stripes to indicate how the concepts are related to the requirements.

4.2 Transformation From the PIM Model to Target Technology

In this stage, an endogenous model-to-model transformation is carried out from the PIM (outputted by the parser) to an enriched PIM that contains the information about the function points estimation explained in Sect. 3. The tool offers two visualizations on top of this enriched PIM: i) Function Points view: and ii)

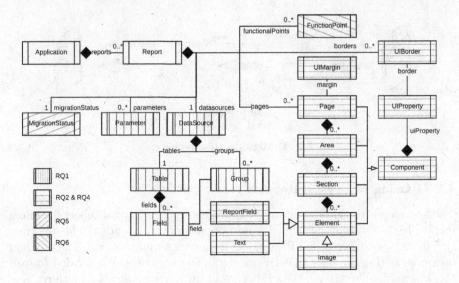

Fig. 2. PIM model

Architecture view (see description below). As soon as developers review/adjust the PIM supported by the views, they launch a model-to-text (M2T) transformation that results in XSL-FO (XSL Format Objects) templates. XSL-FO are files used by Oracle Peoplesoft to parse and render the report data to the output format. We developed the transformations on top of Epsilon languages[4]. It is worth mentioning that we made decisions on the architecture of the target reports to favor performance (RQ3). Such decisions guided us on the M2T transformation development.

4.3   Views and Calculation of Function Points Technology

Based on the model generated in the transformation to PIM ', the calculation of the function points is carried out. To perform this calculation, the EOL language was used, in which the reports are analyzed one by one according to the core structure of the model. In such a way, the necessary logic is implemented according to the method of calculation of function points. This routine is invoked from a java program created on the Epsilon Framework where it executes the EOL routine and generates a .csv file as the output of the process. For the construction of Architecture views and Function Points view were implemented on the Sirius tool, in which table views were generated for Function Points and tree type for editing the object model.

Function Points View. This view (Fig. 3) presents the results of the function point analysis, thus leveraging RQ6. The view has a Grid layout and displays

---

[4] https://www.eclipse.org/epsilon/.

for each report the following information: number of DETs, number of FTRs, level of complexity, number of function points with and without adjustment.

	Dets	Ftrs	Complexity	Points Without Adjustment	Functional Point
Report AJAR3201	61	0	MEDIUM	4	3.28
Report AJFCNAMS	85	3	HIGH	6	4.92
Report AJDEVCLI	23	1	MEDIUM	4	3.28
Report AJINFTRN	13	1	LOW	3	2.46
Report AJLOADCT	24	4	HIGH	6	4.92
Report AJFCREAS	79	5	HIGH	6	4.92
Report INFTRANS	12	1	LOW	3	2.46

Fig. 3. Function points view

As a result of the automation of the calculation of the function point count, the analyzed reports have a variation of complexity from low to high. For example, for the AJAR3201 report, the algorithm proceeds to go through all the grouping nodes (Group) and Fields. This tour indicates that there is a count of 61 fields and without any main grouping, this because it is a report with a single heading but without detail. In such a way that the count for Dets is 61 and Ftrs is 0. Once the Dets and Ftrs have been determined, the complexity level is recorded, this taking the Transaction Complexity table as a guide. For Ftrs 0 and Dets greater than 16, the complexity value is Medium. For the function points without adjustment, refer to the FP by Transaction Complexity table, in which by definition for this exercise the EQ (External Inquiries) category is taken. As a result, we have the value of the function points without adjustment is 4 Applying the processing factor described in Sect. 3, the set point value is found to be 17. Finally, the calculation of function points is determined as follows: Function Points Without Adjustment = 4 Processing Com- plexity Points = 17 Applying the formula Processing Complexity Factor Processing Complexity Factor = 0.82 Function Points = $4 \times 0.82 = 3{,}28$

Architecture View. This view shows the list of reports involved in the migration process as well as the their constituent elements. The view has a tree layout. The tree diagram represents the elements of the PIM model that conform to the concepts Application, Report, DataSource, Group, Table, Field, ReportField, Image, Page, Area, Section and Text. At the left size of Fig. 4, there is an example of two reports displayed in the tree view. At the right side, the reader can found the icons associated to the main concepts of the PIM.

Note that each report has a background color that indicates its migration state. There are three options: i) White represents a *new* report; ii) Green represents a report *in process*; and iii) Red represents that a report contains *errors*. Examples of errors are: a) reports that have more than one data sources, which

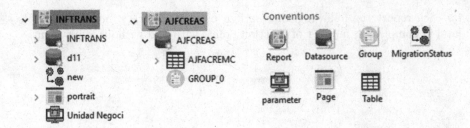

Fig. 4. Architecture view

is out of the migration scope; b) reports containing fields that are in the canvas but not in the datasource.

In addition to the migration status, the architecture view allows developers to perform adjustments on the reports, for example, the introduction of nodes (report, tables, groups) to the tree, in the report customization step. The introduction/deletion of a node could be motivated for two reasons: improve maintainability or usability. Legacy applications contain often plenty of dead code, therefore it is important to provide developers with means to delete dead code. Furthermore, developers could desire to add/delete/update fields to improve user experience.

5   Validation

The purpose of this section is to show that our approach is functional and has no negative impact on the performance of migrated applications. In addition, we present insights about the cost estimation of our tool according to the reports' complexity, and improvements on productivity when using our tool.

5.1   Methodology

The validation is composed of six activities. Firstly, we selected a sample of reports to migrate. Secondly, we applied the migration process to the sample. Then, we checked the functionality of the migrated reports. Next, we run the generated Publisher reports and compared the performance of such reports with that of legacy reports being executed in the production environment. In addition, we analyzed productivity gains in the step of report customization by comparing the time spent when the basic migration has been performed by hand with that of the (semi)automated migration. Finally, we validated that the estimation costs (semi)automatically calculated by our tool were consistent with the report complexity spelt out by a third party. We explain each activity in detail below:

– **Sample selection**: Currently, the company's systems have 212 Crystal Reports with heterogeneous structures, performance and frequency of execution. We wanted to choose a set of reports frequently executed in the company's daily activities. To select them we took into consideration three criteria: average processing time, number of instances executed of a given report, and complexity within the project scope. We took a look at the operation log of the four last months and obtain the number of instances executed and processing time per report. In addition, after reverse-engineering the 212 reports, we checked in the Function Points view that the pre-selected files (those with higher number of instances and longer execution time) were master/detail reports having different levels of complexity, in accordance with RQ1. Thus, we found six files that matched the criteria.

- **Transformation chain and execution of generated reports**: Given a legacy report, the transformation process generates three resources: one model conforming to the PIM metamodel and two target software assets. One of the target resources is the Peopletools project, which has the datasource and the object definitions of the report. Another target resource is the xsl-fo template, which is used by Peoplesoft to render the report data. The next step is to load the generated project into the Peoplesoft environment. This activity creates the reports and datasource definitions, after that, we need to attach the xsl-fo template to its corresponding report definition.
- **Functionality**: After the reports have been migrated, we checked that their functionality remains intact and there is no side effects or missing features after the generation, according to RQ2. This help developers to identify if they need to do something beyond superficial retouches, for example, to recover lost functionality.
- **Performance comparison**: Peoplesoft has a detailed record of the processes that have been run on its environment. We took advantage of this record to identify past performance rates as well as execution parameters. We needed such parameters to execute the migrated reports under the same conditions than legacy and validate the fulfillment of RQ3.
- **Productivity improvements**: We asked the company's development team to estimate the report customization effort after the migration when using a manual approach and when using our tool. Note that even if our tooling automates the migration, developers need to adjust the look-and-feel of generated reports, which is a manual task. In particular, adjustments consist of modifying generated reports to make their graphical structure a mirror of the source Crystal reports (this aspect is aligned with RQ2 too). We compare both estimations to find possible productivity improvements when using our tool, as time reductions in these manual tasks.
- **Estimation accuracy**: We asked a developer of the company (who is not a co-author) to categorize a set of reports according to their complexity. To compare the empirical estimation of complexity made by the developer against the results reported in the Function Points view, we assigned a value in minutes to each function point, according to the experience that we had in the manual migration of a report of low complexity referred to as INFTRANS. For this report, that was manually migrated, we spent 195 minutes. The Function Points view indicated an effort of 2.46 points for this report. Based on this preliminary experiment, we estimated that each function point is equivalent to 79.26 minutes. At this point, we warn that this estimate has a threat to validity. We plan to improve it in the future by carrying out a more robust

experimentation that includes reports of different priorities and the opinion of more than one developer.

5.2   Results

This section presents the results taking into account that the validation aimed at getting insights about four criteria: i) functionality, ii) performance, iii) productivity improvements, and iv) estimation accuracy.

- **Functionality**: The transformation process was successful; each step of the reports migration was completed without exceptions. The generated reports were loaded in the Peoplesoft environment without problems as well.
- **Productivity improvements**: The different steps of a manual migration are: i) initial analysis; ii) datasource definition; iii) report definition; iv) template creation; v) template load; and vi) tests. The team estimated the effort of manually carrying out all of these steps for the sample. In turn, our approach has the following stages: i) automated migration of the essential elements of a report; ii) manual adjustments or customization; iii) tests. We applied our (semi)automated approach to the sample. Whereas the first stage took a very few seconds, steps ii) and iii) took more time. When comparing the effort of the manual approach with that of our approach, we observed that the latter offers productivity gains of 40%.
- **Estimation accuracy**: We compared for each report the estimate of complexity made by a developer against the function points and the estimated minutes automatically obtained by our tool. We found that our tool correctly estimates higher times for reports with more complexity, and lower times for reports with less complexity.
- **Performance**: We compared the performance of the generated reports in the test scenarios with that of the source Crystal reports. Looking at the results one can observe that, except in a case (i.e., the INFTRANS report), the migration from Crystal report to BI Publisher does improve the latency of reports. The reason for the outlier was the server workload and data volume processed by the INFTRANS report in certain runs.

5.3   Discussion

The discussion is organized taking into account the evaluated criteria and the requirements. With respect to functionality, we found that the migration tooling can reverse engineer all reports in the project scope (RQ1), before running the actual transformation towards the target technology. Now, if we look at productivity improvements, we can say that our tooling reduces the migration effort in 40%, which is a good profit for the company. This is mostly due to the fact that generated reports respect architecture principles that ease maintainability and customization tasks, which is not necessary the case in manual migration. However, a post-migration activity –devoted to adjust the templates– currently implies a considerable effort related to graphical interface adjustments. The tool does not put the report fields exactly in the same location of those of the legacy report. As a consequence, developers have to manually modify the location in the XSL-FO template, which allows them to cope with RQ2 but at the same it is time consuming given the file verbosity.

Talking about the performance, the results are quite good (RQ3). In most scenarios, the latency of generated reports is below than that of the legacy reports. Even for most of studied reports, the performance of generated reports is half of the legacy.

With respect to the estimation accuracy (RQ4), we found that our tool correctly estimated times for reports with different complexities. This experiment has a threat to validity: the function point calculation was based on a constant value that was drawn from the manual migration of a low complexity report. Therefore, from this experiment, we cannot guarantee the accuracy of the estimate for higher complexity migrations.

6 Related Work

The reviewed literature falls in two different categories: i) works related to the migration of Crystal Report to newer technologies; and ii) works related to the estimation of function points.

6.1 Crystal Reports Migration

In reviewing the literature we have found: i) a commercial tool for migration of Crystal report reports [3]; ii) two academic approaches to migration of reports in general [2,6].

We categorize the reviewed commercial and academic tools as black-box approaches. The drawbacks of the black-box approach include: i) developers are unaware of the lack of input information needed to the successfully migration and execution of the application in the target technology; ii) the migration progress is unknown to the user; and iii) customization options appears in the final stages of the transformation pipeline [5], thus resulting in tedious and error-prone adjustments that are applied at code level. Based on this fact, the first factor that guided the design of our tool was to find an approach in which the user could see each stage of the transformation, for this reason the tool follows a white-box approximation. Within the academic research, we can highlight that both [2,6] designed a technology-independent model to describe and abstract the concepts of reports in a general way. The models represent the concept of layer, with the aim of decoupling and giving cohesion to each level of functionality. We took inspiration from these works to design our PIM model and the target architecture of reports.

6.2 Function Point Analysis

Lavazza [7] analyzed the Automated Function Points (AFP) standard proposed by the Object Management Group (OMG) to find its benefits and drawbacks.

The AFP specification provides a method to automate the calculation of function points. This method is limited to transaction-oriented applications that use relational databases as persistence unit. AFP uses source code and naming conventions of project files as input for the measurement. In the standard, the source code is transformed to a model representation conforming to the KDM metamodel, which is then translated to a Structured Metrics Meta-model (SMM) that allows the computation of function points [7] found that the AFP specification does not guarantee that the model representation of the source code contains all the functional specifications of the project. Certain elements specified in the International Function Point User Group (IFPUG) standard are not calculated by AFP. As AFP uses source code as an input, the automatic calculations cannot be done for cost estimation purposes in the early stages of the project.

[11] also analyzed AFP and conducted and empirical evaluation of the relationships between FPA and AFP measures and calculation process. Authors found that AFP produces equally accurate and reproducible results as FPA. The differences found between FPA and AFP concern different classification of outputs and the number of files referenced as Internal Logic Files (ILF).

AFP is a robust automated function point analysis method. This method shares the following commonalities with our approach: i) it is limited to transaction-oriented applications; ii) it works for applications that use relational databases as their persistence layer; iii) it excludes certain elements specified in the IFPUG standard; and iv) it does not fully guarantee that the model representation of the source code contains all the functional specifications of the analyzed project.

Instead of using AFP, we decided to propose our own function points analysis approach because we wanted to include the particularities of the legacy technology and prioritize aspects, such as quality attributes, that matters for most of clients of these kind of report applications. We have used the KDM metamodel in previous research [4] and in the context of an MDE course for master students. We have observed two disadvantages: i) it is tough for developers to appropriate the KDM concepts because the metamodel is quite large; ii) some concepts are too abstract, leading developers to different comprehension and application of those concepts, creating confusion in the team. For example, they tend to map the same legacy concept to different KDM concepts that look similar at first glance.

We are aware of the importance of standardization. However, given our interest in smoothing the appropriation of the PIM among practitioners, who are not necessarily MDE experts, we designed an ad-hoc PIM that abstracts only concepts that matter in legacy report technology. Currently our metamodel tackles the concerns of migration technology and function points analysis in the same artifact. However, we consider that the use of a separated metrics metamodel as in AFP is a nice-to-have feature.

7 Conclusion and Future Work

In this work we present an approach and model-based tool support to (semi) automate the modernization of reports from Crystal to BI publisher. This process involved the integration of various Eclipse tools, to address the treatment and transformation of models, where special effort was made to bring the initial terms of the origin technology into a PIM that encompasses the general concepts of Reports. The definition of this PIM makes it possible to abstract concepts which are common to Rapid Application Development (RAD) technologies reports. We believe that even if the metamodel was used in a migration scenario from Crystal to BI Publisher can be reused in other scenarios where the legacy could be other RAD technology such as Oracle Forms, Delphi, etc. This metamodel allows us to construct views on top of it that support developer on decision making on two senses: i) project planning based on effort estimation; and ii) shaping the architecture of reports at model level. The estimate of effort was a factor that was involved in the tool, this estimate was made on the methodology of function points, which allowed us to automate the classification of reports according to their level of complexity. Within the migration process we find that automation saves 40 percent of manual work, giving us advantages while improving the performance of the reports execution. This saving is translated into the reduction of person-hour time of the project and therefore of the costs of the project's development.

Regarding the correctness of the estimation, we found that our tool correctly estimates higher times for reports with more complexity, and lower times for reports with less complexity. It is necessary to conduct a more rigorous experimentation including both : i) a large report dataset with different complexities; and ii) a team of experienced developers who estimate the effort of manual migration for comparison purposes with the tool estimates. This would allow us to adjust the estimation method and the calculation tool.

An additional field of improvement is the graphic distribution of the elements of the report. The current version performs the distribution in a matrix manner in contrast to pixels, leading in some cases to inexact location of elements with respect to the legacy. In reference to this, a view should be added to the approach to allow developers to accommodate the layout, thus facilitating early layout decision making.

References

1. Abrahao, S., Insfran, E.: Early usability evaluation in model driven architecture environments. In: 2006 Sixth International Conference on Quality Software (QSIC 2006), pp. 287–294. IEEE (2006)
2. Cheng, L.Y., Long, H.H., Gan, T.: Research on a agile general report system model based on MDA. In: CCTAE 2010–2010 International Conference on Computer and Communication Technologies in Agriculture Engineering, pp. 305–310 (2010). https://doi.org/10.1109/CCTAE.2010.5544203

3. DataTerrain: DataTerrain Automation - Automated Business Intelligence Reporting Conversion. https://dataterrain.com/reports-conversion/
4. Escobar, D., et al.: Towards the understanding and evolution of monolithic applications as microservices. In: 2016 XLII Latin American Computing Conference (CLEI) (2016)
5. Garcés, K., et al.: White-box modernization of legacy applications: the oracle forms case study. Comput. Stand. Interfaces **57**, 110–122 (2018)
6. Hou, J.: Model-based approach for reporting system development. In: Sun, F., Li, T., Li, H. (eds.) Knowledge Engineering and Management. AISC, vol. 214, pp. 207–215. Springer, Heidelberg (2014). https://doi.org/10.1007/978-3-642-37832-4_19
7. Lavazza, L.: Automated function points: critical evaluation and discussion. In: International Workshop on Emerging Trends in Software Metrics, WETSoM, pp. 35–43 (2015). https://doi.org/10.1109/WETSoM.2015.13
8. Lethbridge, T., Anquetil, N., Erdogmus, H., Tanir, O.: Advances in software engineering. Approaches to Clustering for Program Comprehension and Remodularization, pp. 137–157 (2002)
9. Mendivelso, L.F., Garcés, K., Casallas, R.: Metric-centered and technology-independent architectural views for software comprehension. J. Softw. Eng. Res. Dev. **6**(1), 1–23 (2018). https://doi.org/10.1186/s40411-018-0060-6
10. Parks, N.E.: Testing & quantifying ERP usability. In: Proceedings of the 1st Annual Conference on Research in Information Technology. pp. 31–36. ACM (2012)
11. Quesada-López, C., Madrigal, D., Jenkins, M.: An empirical evaluation of automated function points. In: CIBSE 2016 - XIX Ibero-American Conference on Software Engineering, pp. 214–228 (2016)
12. Symons, C.R.: Function point analysis: difficulties and improvements. IEEE Trans. Softw. Engi. **14**(1), 2–11 (1988)
13. Van Deursen, A., Visser, E., Warmer, J.: Model-driven software evolution: a research agenda. Technical Report Series TUD-SERG-2007-006 (2007)

Evaluation of Work Stealing Algorithms

Juan Sebatían Numpaque and Nicolás Cardozo$^{(\boxtimes)}$ (iD)

Systems and Computing Engineering Department, Universidad de los Andes,
Bogotá, Colombia
{js.numpaque10,n.cardozo}@uniandes.edu.co

Abstract. Work stealing is a common model in parallel computing used
to schedule the execution of tasks. In this model, tasks are assigned
dynamically to different processors as they are generated by a computation. However, to improve execution time, idle processors can steal tasks
from other processors. Different underlying techniques have been proposed for work stealing, with FIFO and LIFO among the most used techniques. In this work we propose an alternative to these techniques, based
on task priority, as a means to avoid fairness problems in the way that tasks
are stolen across processors. To evaluate our technique we use a benchmark of different computation topologies variating the amount of tasks,
the dependance between tasks, and the number of processors used. Our
results show different performances for the three evaluated techniques. In
cases managing smaller computations with fewer processors, both FIFO
and LIFO perform better. When we increase the size of the computations
and the number of processors used, our proposed priority-based technique
performs better. With respect to the fairness of the algorithms, they are
all unbalanced and no significant conclusion can be reached.

Keywords: Parallel computing · Work stealing · Dynamic scheduling

1 Introduction

Modern software systems normally incorporate parallel, cloud, machine-learning,
or big-data technologies in their development. The development of such systems
has risen with the emergence of modern multi-core processors and the advance-
ment in multi-processing algorithms that facilitate development and speedup
their computation.

One of the algorithmic techniques to speedup concurrent computations is that
of dynamic scheduling [6]. In such algorithms, tasks are dynamically assigned
during the execution to each of the available processors. Work stealing algorithms [4,11] are among the most popular approaches for dynamic scheduling.
In work stealing, tasks are not strictly assigned to a unique processor as they are
spawned, instead, tasks are dynamically allocated by considering the number of
available (*i.e.,* idle) processors. The specific algorithm used to choose (*i.e.,* steal)
a task from processors' available task queue may vary (most commonly using
First-in First-out (FIFO) or Last-in First-out (LIFO) policies), which dictates
the scheduler's inner work and performance.

© Springer Nature Switzerland AG 2022
E. Gonzalez et al. (Eds.): CCC 2021, CCIS 1594, pp. 133–150, 2022.
https://doi.org/10.1007/978-3-031-19951-6_9

In this paper we review the classic work stealing algorithms as a means to understand them in depth, with the objective of improving their execution time. To improve the execution time, we propose a new work stealing algorithm based on a priority-based policy, assigning priorities to each task in the computation graph, with respect to their topological order. The idea behind our proposal is that the tasks to execute by available processors are exactly those that come first in the topological order, as many other tasks depend on them to complete their execution.

We focus the evaluation of our proposed priority-based algorithm with respect to the classical algorithms, FIFO and LIFO, from two perspectives, performance and fairness. The performance evaluation focuses on the execution time of different simulated multithreaded computations. Using the same simulation, we evaluate fairness measuring the amount of tasks processed by each processor. Our results show a slight performance improvement for our proposed algorithm, while the behavior of the three algorithms is very similar, and unbalanced, when evaluating fairness.

We start the paper in Sect. 2 providing an outlook and context for work stealing algorithms and discuss the two classical algorithms based on the FIFO and LIFO policies. In Sect. 3 we introduce our proposed priority-based work stealing algorithm. The evaluation of our algorithm, in Sect. 4, presents the execution of our benchmark simulating the execution of different configuration variants for each of the three algorithms. Finally, Sect. 5, presents the conclusion of our work, and offers avenues of future work.

2   Background

This section describes the state-of-the-art and background in work stealing algorithms. We begin by presenting schedulers in multithreaded computations. In second place, we present the model for multithreaded computations used in work stealing schedulers. Finally, we conclude this section presenting the most classic work stealing algorithms.

2.1   Giving Context to Work Stealing

There are many techniques for scheduling aperiodic tasks in multithreading computations [6]. The majority of the work in this area deals with *static scheduling* algorithms, *i.e.*, algorithms that, beforehand, compute which tasks are going to be executed in their corresponding order for each of the processors involved in the computation. One of the major advantages of static scheduling algorithms is their predictability, since, for a given static schedule, it is straightforward to derive information on the application's execution time. However, static scheduling algorithms require precise information on the execution times of the tasks to be scheduled, which are hard to obtain for modern multiprocessor. Moreover, static schedulers heavily depend on the architecture of the machine where the application is going to be executed, which severely affects portability [9].

Unlike static scheduling, *dynamic scheduling* is performed on-the-fly. With the emergence of multiprocessors, dynamic scheduling has gained interest given the fact that many applications create dynamically changing sets of tasks that need to be scheduled among the processors. The main advantages of dynamic scheduling algorithms for multiprocessor systems are the automatic load balancing and improved portability. The downside of using dynamic scheduling is the limited predictability on the execution performance for the overall computation.

Work stealing stands as one of the most widely used approaches for dynamic scheduling. The idea behind work stealing is that an idle processor "steals" work from other randomly chosen processor as a means to accelerate computations. A processor is said to be *idle* if the queue that stores ready tasks (*i.e.*, task ready to execute) is empty. If all processors are busy (their ready task is not empty), then there is no need to migrate tasks between them. Among the benefits of work stealing the following are identified [10]:

- Scalability with respect to the number of processors.
- Idle-initiative task migration minimizes the scheduling overhead.
- Communication overhead is kept low by taking into account data locality.

Work stealing has been employed in many frameworks for parallel programming [3], and has found plenty of applications in simple divide-and-conquer algorithms [5] and complex stream processing applications [2].

2.2   A Model for Multithreaded Computations

Multithreaded computation can be described as a Directed Acyclic Graph (DAG) in which every node represents a unit-size task and each edge models the dependency among these tasks [4]. In this model a task cannot be executed if its parent tasks have not been executed. Moreover, multithreaded computation's DAGs have one root and one sink, representing the first and last tasks in the computation, respectively. Therefore, an execution schedule for a multithreaded computation must obey the constraints imposed by the topology of the DAG representing it.

We quantify and bound the execution time of a multithreaded computation as in Eq. (1). For a given computation, let $T(S)$ denote its execution time, and let T_n be the execution time for a computation with n-processors and schedule S.

$$T_n = \min_{S} T(S). \tag{1}$$

T_1 is the time that it takes one processor to execute all tasks in the computation, and T_∞ is the time to execute the computation using an arbitrarily large number of processors. Note that these quantities are proportional to the number of vertices of the DAG modeling the execution and its longest path respectively. Based on the execution time, a scheduler is said to satisfy the *greedy property* if at each execution step in which at least n tasks are ready, then n tasks execute. If fewer than n tasks are ready, then all execute [4]. We then have the following result bounding greedy schedulers' execution time.

Theorem 1. *(Greedy-Scheduling Theorem). For any multithreaded computation and any greedy schedule $\mathcal{S}$,*

$$T(\mathcal{S}) \leq \frac{T_1}{n} + T_\infty.$$

As mentioned in Sect. 2.1, in a work stealing scheduler, each processor has a *ready dequeue*, which is a double-ended queue that stores tasks to be executed. Processors successively dequeue tasks from its ready dequeue, executes them, and continues with the next task in their ready dequeue. A task may *spawn* new tasks, represented as the children of a given vertex in the DAG modeling the computation. Spawned tasks are enqueued in the ready dequeue of the processor that executed their parent. Note, however, that this does not imply that all parents of the spawned tasks have been executed. If a processor attempts to execute a child task without completing the execution of its parents, then the processor yields a *stalled* state. For example, in Fig. 1, after executing Task 1, the left-most processor spawned four tasks, enqueued in its ready dequeue. If the ready dequeue of a processor is empty (*i.e.*, the processor is idle), it begins work stealing. When work stealing, a processor steals a task from other processor's ready dequeue. In this example, the idle processors steal tasks 2, 3, and 4 from the left-most processor's ready dequeue (Queue A).

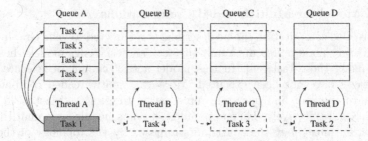

Fig. 1. Work stealing scheduler on a system with four processors [9]

2.3   Work Stealing Policies and Algorithms

In the literature, there are two main algorithms for scheduling multithreaded computations using work stealing which also satisfy the greedy property [4,9]. The main difference between these algorithms is that stealing, local enqueueing and dequeueing is made following either the LIFO or FIFO policies, which we explain now.

In the *LIFO work stealing algorithm* each of the processors executing the computation follows three rules to change their state:

1. **Spawns.** If a processor executes a task that spawns a set of tasks A, each task in A is placed at the bottom of the ready dequeue of the processor. In the next step the processor begins to work on the bottom task.
2. **Stalls.** If a processor stalls, then it checks its ready dequeue and starts working on the bottom task. If the ready dequeue is empty, the processor begins work stealing.
3. **Stealing.** When work stealing, a processor steals the top task from the ready dequeue of a randomly chosen processor and begins working on it. If the victim's ready dequeue is empty, the processor chooses another processor at random.

The main motivation for processors accessing their ready dequeues in LIFO order is that most tasks share data with the task that spawned them. Hence, when a newly created task is executed, it is very likely that the required data is still in the cache of the processor [1]. However, this approach is not *fair* in the sense that a task in the top of the ready dequeue of a processor might never be executed if all worker threads are busy. Thus, there is not guarantee that a run is executed continuously, and there will be no upper bound on the timespan between creation and execution of a task.

In the *FIFO work stealing algorithm*, the proposed solution addresses the fairness problem [9]. If the first enqueued task is the first to execute then there are no tasks perpetually waiting to be executed. The FIFO algorithm is similar to the LIFO algorithm. The main differences between the two algorithms lie in the way of enqueueing, dequeueing, and stealing tasks. The following explains the state change rules for the FIFO-based processors:

1. **Spawns.** Spawned tasks are enqueued at the top of the ready dequeue of the processor. As in the LIFO case, the processor always executes the bottom-most task in its ready dequeue.
2. **Stalls.** Works in the same way as for the LIFO algorithm.
3. **Stealing.** When work stealing, a processor always steals the bottom-most task from other processor's ready dequeue.

3 Priority-Based Work Stealing

The LIFO and FIFO algorithms described before are agnostic to the dependencies between tasks. Our proposal, is to use information on task dependency (*e.g.*, gathered using static analysis) to improve the performance of work stealing schedulers. Our proposal assigns a priority to each task, and steals tasks from other processors based on such priority.

In this section we present the idea behind our priority-based work stealing algorithm, the assignment of priorities based on a DAG structure modeling the computation, and describe the algorithm modeling multithreaded computations.

3.1 Priority-Based Work Stealing

In our analysis of the work stealing algorithms presented in Sect. 2.3, we notice that there is a strong relationship between stalled processors and task dependency. The more tasks depending on the currently enqueued/dequeued tasks, the more processors stall. As tasks that have many children may be potential bottle necks during the execution, they should be given priority when a processor core is dequeuing tasks from its ready dequeue or stealing from other processors.

To solve this problem, we propose a *Priority-based work stealing algorithm*. The motivating idea for our algorithm is to steal, enqueue, and dequeue tasks according to a *priority* assigned to each task in the computation. The priority of tasks depends on how critical is the task for the computation, where the criticality of a task is defined by the amount of subtasks spawned by a task, since these are the tasks more likely to generate bottle necks during the execution. We measure task criticality as the longest path of a vertex describing the task to the sink of the DAG modeling the computation. This metric is reasonable as the longer the path between the vertex and the sink, the more tasks will depend on the task, rising the probability of the task becoming a bottle neck.

A processor running the priority-based work stealing algorithm follows the next rules to change its state:

1. **Spawns.** If a processor executed a task that spawns a set of tasks, A, then the tasks in A are inserted, by priority order, in the processor's ready dequeue. The ready dequeue of every processor is ordered in descending priority order. In the next step, the core begins to work on the bottom task (*i.e.,* the task with the highest priority).
2. **Stalls.** If a processor stalls, then it checks its ready dequeue and starts working on the bottom task. If the ready dequeue is empty, the processor begins work stealing.
3. **Stealing.** When work stealing, a core steals the bottom task from the ready dequeue of a randomly chosen processor and begins working on it. If the victim's ready dequeue is empty, the core tries again picking another core at random.

3.2 Modeling and Implementing Multithreaded Computations

To model a multithreaded computations we use a DAG where each vertex represents a task in the computation, and the out edges of a vertex represent the spawned tasks. In turn, in-edges for a vertex, represent the tasks the vertex depends on. Multithreaded computations are modeled as follows.

Let $G = \langle V, E \rangle$ be a directed graph where V is the set of vertices and E the set of edges between elements in V. Vertices are labeled with the numbers $1, \ldots, N$ and let $A(G)$ be the $V \times V$ adjacency matrix of G such that

$$A(G)_{ij} = \begin{cases} 1 & \text{if there is a directed edge from vertex } i \text{ to vertex } j, \\ 0 & \text{otherwise.} \end{cases}$$

for all $1 \leq i, j \leq N$. Recall that a graph G is a DAG if and only if G admits a topological order. Thus, one can label the vertices of a DAG in such a way that its adjacency matrix is strictly lower triangular.

Conversely, if the adjacency matrix of a graph G is strictly lower triangular, then G is a DAG. We will restrict the application of our algorithm to multi-threaded computations that generate DAGs. Note from our definition, that an adjacency matrix with more than one zero column implies that the DAG has more than one root. Similarly, having more than one zero row implies that the DAG has more than one sink. Neither case is applicable to multithreaded computations.

3.3   Priorities Algorithm

As discussed in Sect. 3.1, we define a work stealing strategy based on a priority function given by the longest path from a vertex to the sink vertex of the DAG modeling the computation. Given two vertices i, j in the DAG, the vertex i will have a higher priority than j if the longest path $lp(i)$ from i is greater than $lp(j)$ from j. Algorithm 1.1 shows how the longest path is computed for all vertices in our computation's DAG [8].

```
void lp(int i) { //compute the longest path for vertex i
  G := ⟨V,E⟩
  int [] priority := new PQ(N) //priority queue of size N=|V|

  if (!priority[i]) {
    //d:V → N longest path for vertex i
    int d(int i) {
      if (i != N)
        return   max(i,j)∈E{d(j) + 1}
      else
        return 0
    }
    for (int i=1; i<=N; i++)
      priority[i] := d(i)
  }
  //priority is filled with the longest paths from each vertex
      of G to the out vertex of the computation
  return priority[i]
}
```

Algorithm 1.1. Priority computation of all the vertices in a DAG modeling a multithreaded computation.

Note from Algorithm 1.1 that it is sufficient to calculate $d(1)$. Vertex 1 is connected to every vertex i, for $1 < i \leq N$, therefore $d(i)$ is calculated recursively for every task spawned once we calculate $d(1)$.

3.4   Priority Work Stealing Scheduler

Given a DAG for a multithreaded computation (*e.g.,* generated from a static analysis tool to extract the structure from the computation), the first step for our work stealing algorithm is to calculate the priorities for all vertices as in Algorithm 1.1. This is done by a multithreaded computation manager component. Then, a work stealing manager component creates an object to manage all the components to manage the computation. That is, managing the ready dequeue for each processor.

The execution starts by choosing the first task (the root node in the DAG) to execute in a given processor (*e.g.,* processor p_0). As processors visit tasks (vertices in the DAG), the multithreaded computation manager marks them as visited and proceeds to search task's children. If the children tasks are not yet enqueued, they are added to the processor's ready dequeue, following the rules of the work stealing algorithm. Then, the processor checks its ready dequeue and executes the next task, the bottom task (according to the rules of the work stealing algorithm). Recall that if all the parents of the task that the processor is attempting to execute have not been executed yet, the processor stalls meaning that it looks in its ready dequeue for another task to execute. If the core fails to find a task ready to execute, it begins work stealing.

Remember a processor begins work stealing if either its ready dequeue is empty or is stalled and fails to find a task ready to execute in its ready dequeue. In this case, the processor informs the multithreaded computation manager that is looking for a vertex to steal. The multithreaded computation manager adds the processor to a pool of processors looking for vertices to steal and puts it on hold. Meanwhile, the work stealing manager looks, among the procesos that are not stealing, for processors that have tasks available in their ready dequeues to steal from. A processor is chosen as victim if it has more than one task in its ready dequeue. In this case it gives to the multithreaded computation manager the bottom task in its ready dequeue. The multithreaded computation manager gives the stolen task to one of the processors in the pool, which, in the next step, attempts to execute the task. If all the processors attempt to steal at the same time, they generate a deadlock. To address this problem, if the number of processors work stealing at any given step equals the number of processors executing the computation, the pool is reset, causing each of the processors to execute the bottom task in their ready dequeue. Given that the execution time of tasks varies, not all processors will reach a stealing state at the same time, allowing for the computation to progress.

To implement the aforementioned process, each of the components described are represented by a Java class, as described in the following.[1]

1. The multithreaded computation manager component implements Algorithm 1.1 to calculate the priority of each vertex in the DAG.

---

[1] Available at our GitHub repository: https://github.com/FLAGlab/WorkStealing Algorithms.

2. A component to update and manage the state of the multithreaded computation. This component knows the number of processors available, which vertices of the DAG have been visited, which vertices are enqueued in the ready dequeue of a processor, and how many of the parents for a vertex have not been executed yet.

3. The work stealing manager component is in charge of synchronizing work stealing among the processors. This is implemented using threads and synchronized procedures.

4. The controller component receives a DAG and the number of available processors, and orchestrates the complete process, managing instances of the other components above.

4   Validation

We evaluate our proposed priority-based work stealing algorithm using a benchmark to compare with the classic FIFO and LIFO based algorithms. We evaluate the performance and processors' load in different computation graph sizes and densities.

4.1   Experimental Design

To measure performance, we define a benchmark with different evaluation scenarios. In each scenario we take into account the average maximum execution time obtained from all processors across five runs, as a means to reduce warm-up or processor clock bias in our results. To measure processors' load we count the number of tasks executed by each processor with respect to the total number of tasks in the computation.

Each validation scenario uses a different computation size (*i.e.*, number of tasks), generating DAGs to represent the computation containing 50, 100, 200, 400, 800, and 1600 nodes in each scenario. Additionally, for each DAG size we evaluate three different graph density values (*i.e.*, the ratio of outgoing edges to nodes) 0.2, 0.5, and 0.8, to observe the impact of the algorithms in different computation settings. Additionally, we vary the number of processors executing the multithreaded computation between 1 (used as the linear baseline) and 96, scaling in powers of 2. For every possible configuration we use the same generated DAG for all runs for each of the three work stealing algorithms, LIFO, FIFO, and priorities.

DAG Generation. All DAGs representing computations used in our evaluation are generated using the following process. The DAG's density takes into account the ratio between the number of edges and the number of vertices in the graph. To manage this, we follow Erdös-Rényi's model for graph construction [7]. In particular, edges are included in the graph with independent probability $0 < p \leq 1$. Algorithm 1.2 describes the DAG generation process. Lines 3–9 follow Erdös-Rényi's algorithm to generate the DAG's adjacency matrix M, for a given random probability p. Lines 10–17 verify that no row in the matrix is zero, as we only allow for a single root and sink nodes in the computation graphs (as stated in Sect. 3.2). In case a zero row is generated, the values are changed following the Erdös-Rényi algorithm.

```
1  let N > 0 && density in 0 < p ≤ 1.
2  int [][] M := new Array(new Array (N))
3  for(int j=0; j<N; j++) {
4     for(int i=0; i<j; i++) {
5        if(probability(p))
6           M[i][j] := 1
7        else if(probability(1−p))
8           M[i][j] := 0
9     }
10    if(isZero(row(j))) {
11       for(int i=0; i<j; i++) {
12          if(probability(p))
13             M[i][j] := 1
14          else if(probability(1−p))
15             M[i][j] := 0
16       }
17    }
18 }
```

Algorithm 1.2. Generate the adjacency matrix for a DAG, modeling a multithreaded computation, with N vertices and density p.

Evaluation Configuration. All our benchmarks ran on a XeonSP G291-281 GPU Server with two RTX2080 CPUs, each with 48 physical cores with a 2.2 GHz frequency and a 128 GB NUMA enabled memory architecture, running the Ubuntu 20.04.2 LTS OS. We use version 1.8 of the JVM for our experiments.

4.2   Results

To evaluate the performance, we take into account the execution time, given in milliseconds, for each of the algorithms, across all DAG sizes for each of the densities. Figures 2 through 13 show the behavior of the three algorithms scaling up the number of processors used.

Our second experiment evaluates the load of each processor when executing a multithreaded computation with a fixed number of tasks and a fixed density for the dependencies between tasks. As mentioned in Sect. 2.3 the original FIFO and LIFO algorithms may be unfair [9] with respect to the way in which processors chose the tasks to execute or steal from other processors. Therefore, the purpose of this experiment is to assess the fairness of our proposed algorithm with respect to the FIFO and LIFO algorithms. Figures 14 through 19, show the number of tasks executed by each processor for a given computation. Here we show the computation of 200 tasks running with 8 and 32 processors respectively, variating

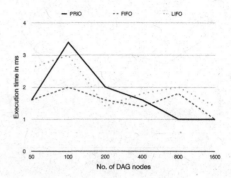

Fig. 2. Algorithms comparison for density 0.2 using 1 processor

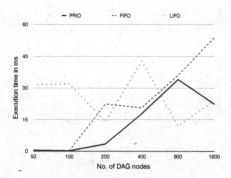

Fig. 3. Algorithms comparison for density 0.2 using 8 processors

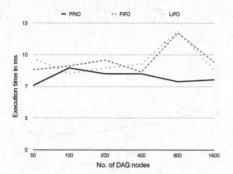

Fig. 4. Algorithms comparison for density 0.2 using 32 processors

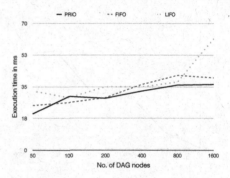

Fig. 5. Algorithms comparison for density 0.2 using 96 processors

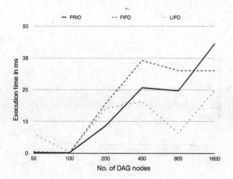

Fig. 6. Algorithms comparison for density 0.5 using 1 processor

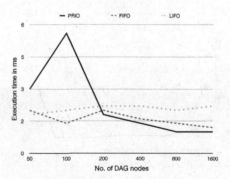

Fig. 7. Algorithms comparison for density 0.5 using 8 processors

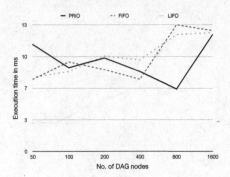

Fig. 8. Algorithms comparison for density 0.5 using 32 processors

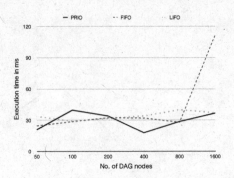

Fig. 9. Algorithms comparison for density 0.5 using 96 processors

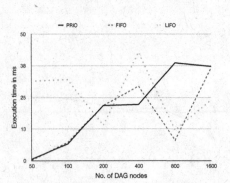

Fig. 10. Algorithms comparison for density 0.8 using 1 processor

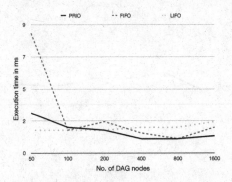

Fig. 11. Algorithms comparison for density 0.8 using 8 processors

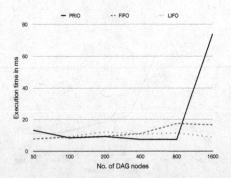

Fig. 12. Algorithms comparison for density 0.8 using 32 processors

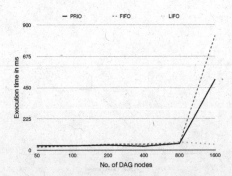

Fig. 13. Algorithms comparison for density 0.8 using 96 processors

the density of dependencies between tasks. Each column shows the number of tasks executed by each of the processors. The behavior of other variations of computation sizes and numbers of processors present a similar behavior, which we present in an online appendix together with all other data and algorithms from our work.[2]

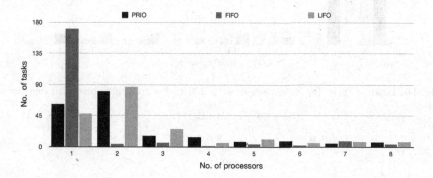

Fig. 14. Load of tasks for 8 processors with 200 task's computations with density of 0.2

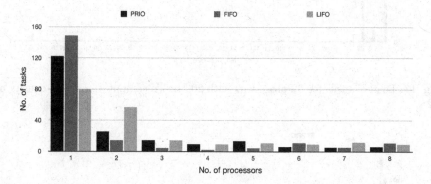

Fig. 15. Load of tasks for 8 processors with 200 task's computations with density of 0.5

4.3   Analysis of the Results

From the performance results we can observe that the behavior of the algorithms is erratic, with individual cases favoring one algorithm over the others. Across all density configurations using fewer processors (*i.e.*, ≤ 8) the best performing algorithm in most cases is FIFO. However, as we increase the number of tasks in the computation (*i.e.*, DAG nodes), and the number of processors, the performance of our proposed algorithm rapidly improves across all configurations. We can

---

[2] https://flaglab.github.io/WorkStealingAlgorithms/.

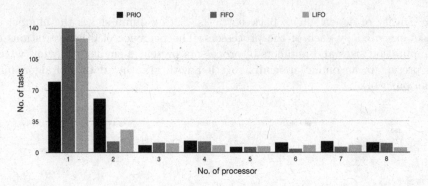

Fig. 16. Load of tasks for 8 processors with 200 task's computations with density of 0.8

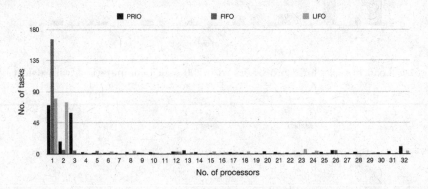

Fig. 17. Load of tasks for 32 processors with 200 task's computations with density of 0.2

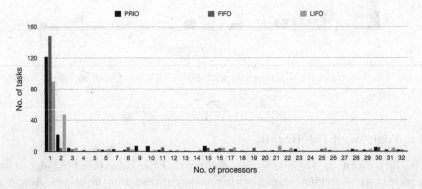

Fig. 18. Load of tasks for 32 processors with 200 task's computations with density of 0.5

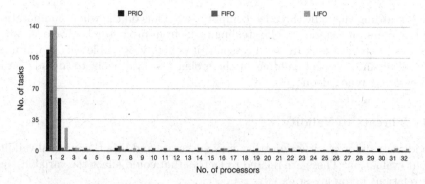

Fig. 19. Load of tasks for 32 processors with 200 task's computations with density of 0.8

observe the FIFO and priority algorithms present a rapid performance decrease around 800 DAG nodes in highly dense graphs with many processors (the last two configurations), while the LIFO algorithm is in average more stable. We also observe that the proposed priority-based algorithm presents a better performance in average than its FIFO and LIFO counterparts in the sparse density scenarios. However, as the density of the graphs and the number of processors used increase, the performance of the three algorithms becomes very similar.

We can observe that the benefit of our proposed priority-based algorithm comes for larger computations as the number of processors used increases (not taking into account outlier performance results for any of the algorithms). Therefore, we argue that for heavy computations including a high level of parallelism, our priority-based algorithm is best suited. When we deal with smaller-size computations, using the base FIFO algorithm can be best suited. However, our evaluation is not conclusive with respect to specific situations in which one of the two classic algorithms triumph the other. The difference in their execution may be due to the specific structure of the underlying DAG for the computation.

In many cases we observe a performance decay as we use 96 processors for the evaluation. This behavior is due to the fact that, as mentioned in Sect. 3.4, our evaluation program for multithreaded computations running with n processors uses $n+2$ threads, where the additional threads are used for managing the overall computation; one controlling the processors, and one controlling the stealing controller. Given the configuration of the machine used for our evaluation has a maximum of 96 physical threads, we overload the machine's capacity, which may cause the observed performance decrement.

With respect to the fairness evaluation (Figs. 14, 15, 16, 17, 18 and 19) we observe that most of the tasks are managed by the first couple of processors across all cases. However, we note that as the computation graphs are denser, the load among the processors is more unbalanced, specially when more processors are available. In particular, most of the tasks execute on processor 1. One possible reason for this is that, for instance, when setting a 0.8 density, after executing the first task, processor 1 enqueues in its ready dequeue 80% of the vertices of the

DAG modeling the multithreaded computation. Thus on the whole computation the remaining processors will be stealing tasks from processor 1. Moreover, after a processor steals a task from processor 1, it is highly probable that it will need to steal again since the children of the stolen task are likely to already be in processor's 1 ready dequeue.

4.4 Threats to Validity

We identify different situations that may add noise and bias the internal validity of our evaluation. These are related to factors that could affect the variables and the relations being investigated.

The generation of the computations DAGs, following Algorithm 1.2, used to simulated our evaluation scenarios may diverge from DAGs modeling a real multithreaded computation. As a matter of fact, to keep the evaluation scenarios simple, we omit additional conditions imposed in the topology of a DAG modeling a multithreaded computation [4] that could have and impact in the overall performance of the algorithms scheduling a real multithreaded computations.

5 Conclusion and Future Work

Multithreaded computations are becoming the norm in modern software systems. Therefore, being able to exploit the best possible performance from the underlying parallel infrastructure, *e.g.,* schedulers, is key for the success of many software systems.

The main goal of our work is to present a review and evaluate existing and new algorithms to schedule multithreaded computations by means of work stealing. As a result, we proposed a new work stealing algorithm based on a priority assigned to each vertex in the DAG modeling a multithreaded computation. The definition of the priority is calculated algorithmically taking into account the importance of tasks to complete the computation. Tasks with required to finish in order to complete other tasks receive a higher priority and therefore should be scheduled more promptly. In order to evaluate and compare the performance of the work stealing algorithms we use a benchmark to simulate and execute multithreaded computations by means of the generation of a DAG representing the computation. We measure the total execution time and the work load of each processor involved in the multithreaded computation for different configurations variating the size of the computation, the density of interactions between tasks in the computation, and the number of processors used to execute the computation.

Our results show that the proposed algorithm is effective in executing multithreaded computations based on it performance in comparison to the execution of the FIFO and LIFO-based algorithms. Our algorithm shows most useful for larger computations using more processors, while both FIFO and LIFO perform better for smaller-size computations using fewer processors. Our evaluation also shows that the three algorithms are unbalanced, executing most tasks on the first couple of processors and leaving all other processors to manage only a hand full of tasks. In some cases our priority-based presents a better balance than the FIFO and LIFO algorithms, nonetheless, the difference is not significant.

There is no perfect or definitive work stealing algorithm that is best suited for any multithreaded computation. As the results, shown in Sect. 4.2, indicate there are run configurations in which the FIFO presents a better performance, the same way LIFO and priority based do for other configurations. This suggests that there are conditions in the topology of the DAG and the number of processors used to run the multithreaded computation that may favor one algorithm over another. These conditions should be explored as future work.

Our Priority-based work stealing algorithm is not optimally efficient yet. There are improvements that could be made in the priority function in which this algorithm is based to get a better performance. For instance, instead of calculating the priorities of the vertices with the longest path, we can think of calculating them with the number of vertices in their spanning tree. Alternatively, if the DAG we are considering is weighted, the edge's weights are yet another variable to be considered when defining the priority function. A more in-depth evaluation to explore this is needed.

Finally, we could improve or explore alternatives to our priority-based work stealing algorithm by using a graph-theoretical approach to improve and refine the priority function, in which this algorithm is based.

References

1. Acar, U.A., Blelloch, G.E., Blumofe, R.D.: The data locality of work stealing. In: Proceedings of the twelfth annual ACM symposium on Parallel algorithms and architectures, pp. 1–12. SPAA 2000, ACM, New York (2000). https://doi.org/10.1145/341800.341801
2. Anselmi, J., Gaujal, B.: Performance evaluation of work stealing for streaming applications. In: Abdelzaher, T., Raynal, M., Santoro, N. (eds.) Principles of Distributed Systems, pp. 18–32. Springer (2009)
3. Blumofe, R.D., Joerg, C.F., Kuszmaul, B.C., Leiserson, C.E., Randall, K.H., Zhou, Y.: Cilk: an efficient multithreaded runtime system. In: Proceedings of the ACM SIGPLAN Symposium on Principles and Practice of Parallel Programming, pp. 207–216. PPOPP 1595, ACM, New York (1995). https://doi.org/10.1145/209936.209958
4. Blumofe, R.D., Leiserson, C.E.: Scheduling multithreaded computations by work stealing. J. ACM 46(5), 720–748 (1999). https://doi.org/10.1145/324133.324234
5. Cormen, T.H., Leiserson, C.E., Rivest, R.L., Stein, C.: Introduction to Algorithms, Third Edition. The MIT Press, 3rd edn. (2009)
6. Davis, R.I., Burns, A.: A survey of hard real-time scheduling for multiprocessor systems. ACM Comput. Surv. 43(4), 1–44 (2011). https://doi.org/10.1145/1978802.1978814
7. Erdös, P., Rényi, A.: On random graphs I. Publicationes Math. 6, 290–297 (1959)
8. Khan, M.: Lecture notes for the course CSE-221 Graduate Operating Systems (2011)

9. Mattheis, S., Schuele, T., Raabe, A., Henties, T., Gleim, U.: Work stealing strategies for parallel stream processing in soft real-time systems. In: Herkersdorf, A., Römer, K., Brinkschulte, U. (eds.) ARCS 2012. LNCS, vol. 7179, pp. 172–183. Springer, Heidelberg (2012). https://doi.org/10.1007/978-3-642-28293-5_15

10. Neill, D., Wierman, A.: On the benefits of work stealing in shared-memory multiprocessors. Carnegie Mellon University, Tech. rep. (2010)

11. Yang, J., He, Q.: Scheduling parallel computations by work stealing: a survey. Int. J. Parallel Program. **46**(2), 173–197 (2017). https://doi.org/10.1007/s10766-016-0484-8

Analysis of the User Experience for an Application Proposal Oriented to the General Medical Consultation Service

Brayan Tabares Hidalgo[✉] [ID], Michelle Quintero Hernandez[✉] [ID],
Jose Manuel Rojas Tovar[✉] [ID], and Maria Lili Villegas Ramirez[✉] [ID]

University of Quindío, Quindío, Colombia
{btabaresh,msquinteroh,jmrojast}@uqvirtual.edu.co,
mlvillegas@uniquindio.edu.co

Abstract. It has been shown that despite the growing number of applications focused on eHealth, there are few studies related to usability evaluations on this kind of applications. The present report seeks to provide this type of information by analyzing the experience of a set of users when interacting with a prototype for an application focused on attending the remote pre-paid general medical consultation service. The usability of the prototype that is designed is evaluated using a user-centered design methodology. The development of this research in turn generates a design description of the prototype used for the research, which provides a base product for future prototype improvements and usability assessments. The data captured during the tests demonstrated a high level of satisfaction and overall effective usability over the generated prototype. Therefore, both the prototype and the applied methodology are considered feasible for the development of future eHealth applications.

Keywords: Human-computer interaction · General medical consultation · User experience in health

1 Introduction

Within the health promoting entities or EPS in Colombia, it has been identified that one of the services most used by users of these services corresponds to the consultation of general medicine in 77% [1] compared to others. This makes general medical practice a focus of attention when assessing the delivery of health services according to the opinion of the majority of users. On the other hand, improvements in communication technologies focused on health services have produced a significant increase in the quality of life of many populations around the world [2]. eHealth is a technology that covers all forms of electronic healthcare, which is provided over the Internet [3]. In Colombia, different eHealth applications that allow the use of this technology in the health field in the country have been developed [4, 5]. However, it has been identified that the health systems used suffer from a number of problems, including insufficient usability in meeting users' needs for these applications [6]. Additionally, it was found

© Springer Nature Switzerland AG 2022
E. Gonzalez et al. (Eds.): CCC 2021, CCIS 1594, pp. 151–163, 2022.
https://doi.org/10.1007/978-3-031-19951-6_10

that studies focused on analyzing usability while these tools are implemented, are scarce in the Colombian territory. Therefore, this research aims to provide new information through the analysis of the results derived from evaluations with users, through the use of an application proposal aimed at attending general prepaid medical care remotely. It is intended to design the application based on the needs of users, collected through the opinion of some of them, a model developed by researchers on general in-person medical care and existing eHealth applications. To achieve this objective, a methodology derived mainly from the user-centered design (UCD) and roadmap of the article "HCI Incorporation" [7] is used. The latter originally focused on teaching-learning user graphic inter-faces to favor the productive sector of the software industry. The execution of this analysis is expected to contribute to the field of human-computer interaction, focused on general remote medical care in Colombia. This could be reflected in future studies or implementations of tools that need to delve into the elements that interact with users and meet their needs.

During the article, the term "user-patient" is mentioned to refer to the person attended by a medical professional throughout the process of providing health service. Below, four sections are presented in which some related works are documented, the methodology used during the investigation is detailed, the results are documented with the execution of the different phases raised, and the article is concluded.

2   Related Jobs

For the development of this research, a study of the works related to eHealth and the usability of applications was carried out, with other works in which applications developed with the objective of contributing to the health sector are described. Below is a description and analysis of these proposals together with their contribution to the current research.

2.1   Usability of Health Information Systems Within Critical Care Scenarios: A Study of Colombian Highly Complex IPS Clinical History Systems

In this thesis carried out by Fuentes, they propose the elaboration of an evaluation of usability for electronic medical records systems. During the study, doctors' perception of this type of technology was assessed and demonstrated an unsatisfactory level of usability [6]. According to the thesis, this article uses the contextualization of the process and the perception of target users as important factors to take into account when developing applications for health.

2.2   Methods of Usability Testing in the Development of eHealth Applications: A Scoping Review

The purpose of this work by Maramba is to collect, through a selection of related articles between 2014 and 2017, information on empirical methods used in usability testing for eHealth applications. The results of the work report on the scarcity of studies on usability assessments of such applications, as well as the importance of the use of different evaluation methods in evaluating the usability of an eHealth application [8]. During this article, the aim is to contribute and comply with the aforementioned points, by developing the proposed methodology based on user-centered design.

2.3 A Review of Usability Evaluation Methods and Their Use for Testing eHealth HIV Interventions

In this article by Davis, information is collected about usability evaluation methods in technological applications for the health field, applied in patients with HIV [9]. This article serves as a guide for the development of new platforms focused on eHealth. Likewise, it allows knowing the methodologies and selecting one or a set of them to be applied later on a platform like the one developed in this article.

3 Methodology

This project proposes a methodology based on the synthesis of various standards and software artifacts. These include the user-centered design philosophy (UCD) structured in ISO 13407; the review of software requirements of IEEE 1028; the roadmap for teaching-learning design of graphical user interfaces [7]; and artifacts for the design of software used internally by the research group SINFOCI of the University of Quindío. The proposed methodology has been divided into four phases, which are presented below.

3.1 Characterization Phase

A systematic review protocol is initially implemented at this stage. Subsequently, based on the results of the review and the personal experience of the research team, we proceeded to define a version of the face-to-face general medical care model in Colombia. That version was made taking shape in a visual representation, based on a template provided by the University of Quindío, called vivid scenario that runs through the entire process. Next to the scenario, the workflows (customer journey) carried out in the context of the general medical consultation are defined.

3.2 Requirement Analysis Phase

In order to validate the vivid scenario, a survey designed by the research team is conducted based on what is defined by IEEE 1028 and ISO 13407 for the review of software requirements and the evaluation of usability of the proposed model. In addition, the artifacts produced are evaluated by a medical doctor through an interview, from which corrections and recommendations are obtained. Finally, a benchmarking study is carried out for the collection of software requirements, documenting all the information acquired in this phase.

3.3 Design Phase

During this phase, the design of the technological solution is developed based on the two previous phases of characterization and collection of requirements. This takes into account all the recommendations of the survey carried out, and the relevant features required for an eHealth application.

3.4 Testing Phase

In this phase, the prototype is evaluated with users using indicators and tools chosen by the team to capture follow-up variables on the interaction of respondents with the application. These variables will then be compared with those of one of the authors, presenting the latter as optimal performance. A maximum percentage difference of 30% is established in the follow-up variables with respect to the optimal performance, to consider the usable application. In addition to the evaluation, a satisfaction survey is developed that measures the Customer Effort Score (CES), the Customer Satisfaction Score (CSAT) and the Net Promoter Score (NPS) [10]. Finalizing the documentation of the results obtained.

4 Results

This section describes the results of the project following the phases specified in the methodology section (Sect. 3).

4.1 Characterization Phase

A systematic review protocol was proposed where information about the prepaid general medical consultation process was collected. It reviewed books, articles and other sources of information related to the contextualization of the medical care process in Colombia over the year 2005. Google Scholar and websites of health entities were used as the main sources of information.

Some keywords used in different combinations for the search are: "eHealth", "Health care model", "Medical consultation procedure", "Tele-health", "Usability" and "General Medicine". The results of the review yielded concepts, indicators, statistics, and protocols useful for the development of research. Among them is the document "Outpatient consultation procedure" [11] belonging to the municipal E.S.E. Manuel Castro Tovar where activities, descriptions, and people involved are defined during the course of the medical and dental consultation. All the information obtained was documented and a version of the general medical care model in Colombia was developed. The process represents two sub-processes corresponding to the admission and delivery of the health service, focusing mainly on the transfer of information between the parties involved.

Next, the resulting model. The user goes to the receptionist, where it verifies the data and identification of the user. Afterwards, the receptionist verifies the existence of the consultation in the pre-programmed agenda and tells the patient to wait for his appointment. The healthcare professional then calls the patient to the office and begins the medical care process. During the process, the doctor obtains the medical history, the reason for the consultation, the current illnesses and the symptoms that the patient suffers. The doctor then performs the anamnesis on the patient in order to find a diagnosis. Then, the doctor takes the vital signs and anthropometric measurements, typing the results in the medical history. Subsequently, the doctor interprets all the information and generates the diagnosis, which he communicates in detail to the patient and digits in the clinical history. Then, the healthcare professional makes the medical examination orders and/or prescription medications according to the diagnosis and are explained to the patient. Finally, the doctor makes observations about the next step to follow and other recommendations that are communicated to the patient and recorded in the clinical history. We make use of different artifacts where it is allowed to organize and visualize the information collected.

Characterization Artifacts. An artifact called a vivid scenario that allows the process carried out during a prepaid general medical consultation to be represented using isometric figures was developed (see Fig. 1).

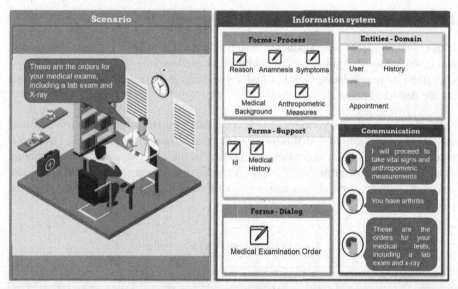

Fig. 1. Capture of the vivid scenario "Procedure of general medical consultation". This image has been made using resources from Freepik.com, designed by Macrovector.

This artifact is used internally by the research group SINFOCI of the University of Quindío. The scenario took shape from the point of view of the user-patient, simulating the interaction with the reception and the general practitioner. The document was made according to articles collected concerning the performance of the medical consultation process, the care model defined previously and the experiences of present researchers. In the scenario, a classification is made for each of the forms present in the course of the procedure. "Process forms" classification are those that collect the information that is processed by the user-patient during the process, such as the reason for the consultation and the symptoms. "Dialog forms" represent the information given to the user by the healthcare professional, such as the order for medical examinations. "Support forms" are documents that contain previously acquired information needed for the process, such as the user ID and medical history.

At the top right are the domain entities, referring to the places where information is stored or collected physically during the process. In this section, the "User" entity is used to protect the user's personal information. The "History" entity protects the information captured by the healthcare professional as the medical history of a user. The "Appointments" entity is composed of the information that manages the scheduling of medical appointments. Finally, the bottom right section contains a record of the oral conversation between the user and all other parties involved in the process.

We also used the device called "Customer Journey", which presents sequentially, the flow of the activities carried out during the course of the consultation. There it is possible to clarify in a visual way, about the person responsible for each activity and form, as the life cycle of the care process progresses.

4.2 Requirement Analysis Phase

In this phase, a survey was conducted for the validation of the process and collection of functional software requirements. In addition, a benchmarking study was carried out to strengthen the requirements based on real applications in the market. The studies carried out are described below.

Validation Survey. The vivid scenario was validated with the support of a form created with the Google Forms tool. In this form, we prepared 26 questions (see Table 1), divided into seven sections, each according to a portion of the vivid scenario. These sections were: appointment confirmation; symptoms and history; anamnesis; taking of vital signs and measurements; formulation and delivery of diagnosis; and provision of service in general.

Table 1. Some questions asked in the compilation form.

N°	Question	Goal
6	Do you feel satisfied with the interaction you normally have with your doctor when communicating your symptoms and history? Why?	Satisfaction of conventional service
11	What information is normally requested from you by your doctor during the consultation process?	Compilation of requirements

(continued)

Table 1. (*continued*)

N°	Question	Goal
21	Do you believe that the vivid scenario presented correctly represents the process by which the medical formulation is performed and the delivery of the diagnosis?	Validation of the vivid scenario
26	What aspects of such a face-to-face consultation would you like to find, in one supported by information and communication technologies?	Compilation of requirements

As a population for the survey, people who claim to be familiar with attending general medical consultations were randomly selected, checking this requirement in the form of a question before submitting the form. The form was answered by 23 participants, from whom no information was collected that could create a link between the person and the responses. The questions were asked based on some points in IEEE 1028 and ISO 13407. In each section of the form that was presented to respondents was a question to verify how accurate the vivid scenario created by the research team to simulate the admission and medical care process was.

The survey results show that 95.7% (twenty-two people) of the respondents believe that the vivid scenario correctly represents the appointment confirmation process. All the questions that involved the evaluation of the vivid scenario's representation presented mostly positive answers. For those respondents who did not see the process represented correctly, they were asked to justify their response. All observations were recorded. Later, a meeting was held via Google Meet with a healthcare professional, which validated the stage lived and the structure of the process. All observations documented and the vivid scenario modified.

Software Requirements for Similar Applications. A benchmarking study was carried out with the objective of obtaining information about the market of applications oriented to the health sector, as well as to obtain a list of common functional requirements in this type of technologies. Applications that apply eHealth at any scale and regardless of their focus, that have an Android architecture, and are available in the Google Play or Play Store, were consulted. In total, 17 applications were selected, including ZocDoc, Health Log, Health Tap and Virtual Health. Each of them was observed manually, obtaining the most outstanding features and services available to users of these applications. We obtained 16 features, of which we highlight the ability to schedule, search bar, session system, appointment reminders, appointment calendar, drug control, chat, among others. According to the application study, some of the most noteworthy features for the development of the application prototype were selected manually. Some features were selected prioritizing the objective of bringing the prototype closer to a real application, and discarding features that do not directly influence the consultation process.

4.3 Design Phase

According to the information gathered throughout the characterization phase and the experience of the face-to-face care model, a mock-up application was designed with the help of the Google Slides tool. The application meets the basic functional requirements, in addition to bonuses features and recommendations compiled from user evaluations, interviews with some medical professionals, and features of other applications that are already on the market. Among them, one of the most notable features added to this mockup is the optional function of collecting previously the user-patient information that is required in the described process, without requiring the presence of the healthcare professional. These features were compiled with the goal to allow attending the general medical care service remotely according to features mentioned largely by normal users and verified by the healthcare professional.

The mock-up was designed solely from the user-patient point of view. This prototype allows the user to log in with a pre-existing account and has an interactive password recovery feature. As the main screen, the application offers an agenda feature, where all appointments assigned to the user are listed and ordered by date, along with information about each one of them. At the moment of the appointment, the user joins through the agenda, selecting the correspondent appointment on the list. Then, the user chooses from the various predefined consultation reasons, where it is required to choose one to continue (see Fig. 2).

Fig. 2. Captures of the mock-up for remote general medical consultation, showing sign in, agenda and consultation reason screens.

In the following two screens, the user chooses respectively the symptoms and medical background from a predefined list. Both screens have a search engine and a help button on each component of the list to clarify the meaning of unknowing words by the user. In case that the desired symptom or medical background is not in the list, it is allowed to select the option "Other" that will be questioned later on following screens.

In the next screen, it is possible to enter optionally anthropometric measures and vital constants that are known by the user at the time of the appointment. These measures include height, weight, blood pressure, and body temperature. Finally, on the last screen, the app has a chat where the application makes questions automatically, asking pre-assigned questions about the medical background, symptoms, and measurements that the user previously selected and wrote. Once the information is collected, it is possible to talk to the healthcare professional in charge of providing the general medical consultation service through the same chat. The healthcare professional is notified of all the information acquired by the application questions and the reasons for consultation, medical background, symptoms, and measurements previously typed by the user, thus facilitating the task of information collection. From this point, the application allows the transfer of text, images, and documents between the user and the medical professional until the end of the consultation through the same chat. Figure 3 shows the design of the application prototype, simulating a user's interaction with it, during the medical care process.

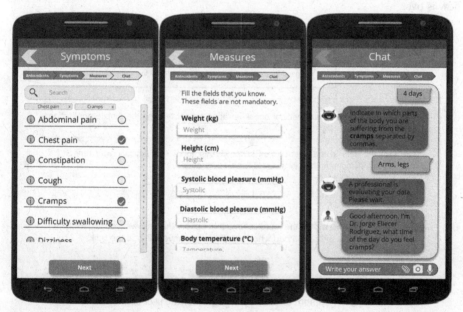

Fig. 3. Captures of the mock-up for remote general medical consultation, showing symptoms, measures and chat screens.

4.4 Testing Phase

Initially, a list of indicators was developed that were used to manually assess the performance of each respondent during the tests, according to the researchers' criteria, and among other aspects that are not allowed to directly question the participants. A sum of 46 context-dependent indicators were produced on the screen in which they occur (see Table 2).

Table 2. Some of the indicators assessed for each of the participants.

N°	Indicator	Screen
2	Does the user move the pointer erratically?	Sign In
7	Does the user seem confused and disoriented?	Agenda
23	Does the user understand when he has selected a symptom?	Symptoms

Additionally, each participant was given a contextualization of how to use the proto-type within Google Slides through mouse interaction exercises. This contextualization puts respondents in the role of a user attending a remote general medical consultation through the application (see Fig. 4). The consultation process was divided into three streams, where each participant is asked to use a vocal alert at the time that they feel the flow is over.

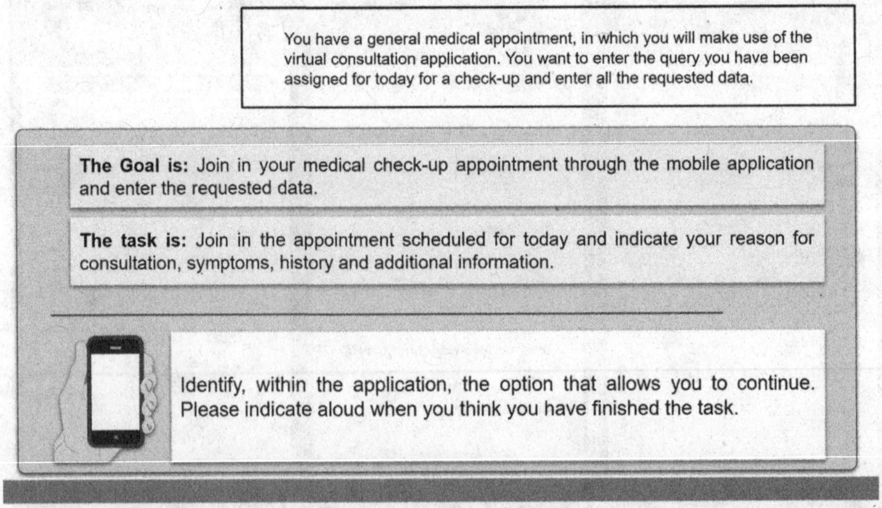

You have a general medical appointment, in which you will make use of the virtual consultation application. You want to enter the query you have been assigned for today for a check-up and enter all the requested data.

The Goal is: Join in your medical check-up appointment through the mobile application and enter the requested data.

The task is: Join in the appointment scheduled for today and indicate your reason for consultation, symptoms, history and additional information.

Identify, within the application, the option that allows you to continue. Please indicate aloud when you think you have finished the task.

Fig. 4. Capture of one of the guides for the user context.

Each evaluation of the prototype was carried out individually and recorded with the respondent's consent for the analysis of the indicators and other components. Once completed, each participant was given an anonymous satisfaction survey, which evaluates the different customer satisfaction indicators such as CES, CSAT and NPS [10]. The assessment scores on a scale between one and five, with one representing the lowest score or if the user disagree with the statement, and five representing the highest score or if the user agree completely with the statement. An amount of 15 questions were made to understand factors like the user feeling while he was browsing through the application (see Table 3).

Table 3. Some of the questions asked on the satisfaction form.

No	Question	Goal
2	Do you think the system is easy to use?	Customer Effort Score (CES)
11	Are you satisfied with the use of this system?	Customer Satisfaction Scale (CSAT)
15	Would you recommend an actual implementation of this system to your friends and acquaintances?	Promoter Net Score (NPS)

Each of the respondents was selected by the research team, creating a mainly young profile composed of university students from diverse academic spaces with an average age of 21 years. Regarding the consistency, ease of use and inclination to reuse the presented application, 100% (Five respondents) said that the application complied with these three components. Although all respondents found the application user-friendly, 20% of them consider the support of a more technical person for its use to be relevant, which suggests that there is still room for improvement of the application flow. 100% of the participants said they were familiar with the prototype and perceived it intuitively. In addition, 80% of respondents consider the prototype to be easy to use. In terms of functionality and usefulness, 20% of respondents agree and 60% more are very agreeing that prototyping can help improve the performance of a general medical practice. The use of avatars in the chat showed a positive reaction in 80% of the respondents, and in a milder way in the remaining 20%.

According to the series of indicators evaluated by the researchers, we analyzed the performance and visible confusion of each of the respondents while navigating the prototype. In the results of these indicators, a minimum level of confusion was found in few users when interacting with the Google Slides tool, especially in the interaction with the Symptoms and Background screens. However, it was found that the vast majority of respondents correctly understood how to interact with input fields, being a vital factor in the process. According to these results, user behavior is considered acceptable, susceptible to improvements to increase the intuitive factor of the application.

With respect to the information captured during the interaction with the prototype, a variable comparison was made (see Table 4). This comparison was between the follow-up variables of each of the participants (P1, P2, P3, P4 and P5) and the same variables while one of the authors performs the tests (P0).

Table 4. Monitoring variables captured during testing.

	P0	P1	P2	P3	P4	P5	Average P1–P5
Pixels	51022	51315	61871	83457	63721	69598	65992,40
Clicks	42	43	45	65	53	61	51,67
Time (Minutes)	2,9	3,2	3,02	3,33	3,10	4,02	3,26

Among the variables captured are the number of pixels traversed by the mouse, the number of clicks made, and the total time spent in resolving the application flows. As a result, it was observed that participants averaged 29% more pixels with the mouse, made 22% more clicks in the application and took 12% more to perform the same task. The results were considered positive because the average follow-up percentages have a variation less than the maximum 30% established in the research methodology.

5 Conclusions and Future Works

Following the analysis of the data collected during the evaluations, there is a high level of acceptance, a slight ease of use and a minimum level of effort on the part of users in this application proposal. Therefore, the methodology applied with the objective of guaranteeing usability and mainly satisfying the needs of the user-patient, demonstrates to have effective results when designing an application in the area of eHealth. In accordance with the above, it is considered opportune to develop future applications of this type using design methodologies similar to the one proposed here, where the satisfaction and the needs of the user-patient take a fundamental role in the elaboration of the same. It is advisable to deepen in an evaluation with more participants under a prototype corrected and implemented in code, this in order to obtain data on a larger scale to compare them with the results of this research. Additionally, it is recommended to study the experience that an application such as the proposal could present on the other roles involved in the process.

References

1. Colombia: Ministerio de Salud y Protección Social "Informe al Congreso de la República 2018–2019", pp. 96–99. Planning of Sector Studies, Bogotá D.C., July 2019
2. Moser, I.: Tecnologías y nuevas relaciones en el cuidado, vol. 3, no. 1. Col·legi Oficial d'Infermeres i Infermers de Barcelona, Barcelona (2019)
3. Oh, H., Rizo, C., Enkin, M., Jadad, A.: What is eHealth (3): a systematic review of published definitions. J. Med. Internet Res. **7**(1), 1–12 (2005)
4. Quispe-Juli, C.U., Moquillaza-Alcántara, V.H., Arapa-Apaza, K.L.: Telehealth in latin america: a review of the studies registered in clinicaltrials.gov. Rev. Cuba. Inf. en Ciencias la Salud **30**(4), 1–12 (2019). https://doi.org/10.36512/rcics.v30i4.1389.g871

5. Cadavid Rengifo, H.F.: E-health y m-health en Colombia: antecedentes, restricciones y consideraciones para el desarrollo de nuevas tecnologías basadas en software. Rev. la Esc. Colomb. Ing. **109**, 89–99 (2018)
6. Fuentes Morán, Y.M.: Usabilidad de los sistemas de información en salud dentro de escenarios de atención crítica: un estudio de los sistemas de historia clínica en IPS de alta complejidad colombianas, Universidad Nacional de Colombia, Bogotá (2013)
7. Giraldo, W., Villegas, M.L., Collazos, C.: Incorporación de HCI: Modelo de Ecosistema, Eje Cafetero Colombia. In: CHIJOTE 2018 – II Jorn. Trab. sobre Enseñanza HCI, September 2018, Universitat de Lleida, pp. 63–69 (2018)
8. Maramba, I., Chatterjee, A., Newman, C.: Methods of usability testing in the development of eHealth applications: a scoping review. Int. J. Med. Inform. **126**, 95–104 (2019). https://doi.org/10.1016/j.ijmedinf.2019.03.018
9. Davis, R., Gardner, J., Schnall, R.: A review of usability evaluation methods and their use for testing eHealth HIV interventions. Curr. HIV/AIDS Rep. **17**(3), 203–218 (2020). https://doi.org/10.1007/s11904-020-00493-3
10. Bustamante Lazcano, J.A.: Métodos de recolección de información para el análisis de la satisfacción del cliente. Ixmati, n.° 8, pp. 27–34, Apr 2021
11. Calderón, L.A.: Procedimiento de Consulta Ambulatoria. E.S.E. Manuel Castro Tovar, Huila, Colombia, Cod. SA-P-001 v2 (2015)

Author Index

Printed in the United States
by Baker & Taylor Publisher Services

Printed in the United States
by Baker & Taylor Publisher Services